All For Show
Television and Film Scripts

All For Show

Television and Film Scripts

Written By
Mary Michelle Jefferson

Edited By
Mylia Tiye Mal Jaza

**All For Show:
Television and Film Scripts**

Copyright © 2007 Mary Michelle Jefferson
All Rights Reserved.

This collection of plays is a presentation of works of fiction. No part of this book may be reproduced or transmitted in any form or by any means (graphic, electronic, or mechanical - including photocopying, recording, taping, or by any information storage retrieval system existing or hereafter invented) without the written permission of both author and publisher.

BePublished.Org
(972) 880-8316

For Information Address:
mari@bepublished.org
THE CONGLOMERATE - BePublished
1601 Garnet Ln., #3403
Fort Worth, TX 76112
(817) 446-7280

ISBN: 978-0-6151-6331-4

Printed in the United States of America

First Edition

All For Show: Television and Film Scripts

TABLE OF CONTENTS

SCREENPLAY

Love Changes

Page 3

SITCOM

Mixed: I Knew I Had It

Page 151

NOTES

Author Bio

Page 195

All For Show: Television and Film Scripts

All For Show: Television and Film Scripts

SCREENPLAY

LOVE CHANGES

FADE IN

INT. APARTMENT BUILDING ELEVATOR - NIGHT

The elevator door opens and Unit 468 is approached.

Fumbling keys JINGLE.

The door is unlocked and opened.

Entering the apartment, boxes with and without labels are seen on the floor and counters, and are stacked against walls that still have photographs hanging.

INT. APARTMENT - NIGHT

The DOOR SHUT is loud. The two lock CLICKS are softer.

                FEMALE
            (raised voice)
        GM! Love! You home?

A young Anglo man wearing a security uniform steps from a room to the right of the short hallway.

                GM
        Right here Bliss baby.

GERALD folds the T-shirt in his hand, and steps back into the room - continuing to talk to BLISS and slightly increasing the volume of his voice.

                GM
        The movers are already en route
        to get me out of here. What was
        the hold up, traffic?

                BLISS
        Wrong question. Do you need me
        to go through and pack what you
        haven't gotten to yet?

(cont'd)

(cont'd)

A trophy is noticed among many plaques and other trophies.

The trophy is inscribed "Supervisor of the Year, Gerald Ma'Xiggio."

> GM
> There's not really much to do, but you can start anywhere up there and I'll keep working back here.

Bliss hears a THUMP and looks at the hallway.

Out comes GM (GERALD) from the room wiping his hands on a green towel and walking toward Bliss saying to her:

> GERALD
> How could I have neglected to kiss the queen of both the Nile and the Mississippi? The fire from your presence spreads throughout the room every time you enter, no matter where you are.

Bliss GIGGLES.

A mirror reflects Gerald kissing on a young African-American woman wearing jeans and a "Happy to be Nappy" t-shirt.

Bliss hugs him with pats on the back and then says:

> BLISS
> I know how you can be . . . engulfed and prone to get tunnel vision. I know you love me and am glad I'm here.

The door bell RINGS.

(cont'd)

(cont'd)

>   GERALD
>   One quick kiss, Bliss?
>
>   BLISS
>   Not before the wedding, Nut.
>   Now get the door.

Gerald walks from Bliss toward the door and is LAUGHING.

Bliss begins removing pictures from the wall.

Gerald talks with movers and Bliss packs and daydreams.

EXT. WEDDING WITH OCEAN AND MOUNTAINS IN BACKGROUND - DAY

A variety of flower types and colors are seen on an arch, on tree trunks and branches, and on the diverse wedding party.

Two white doves are released and bubbles are blown by wedding guests who are also RINGING BELLS.

>   GERALD
>   I love you Bliss.
>
>   BLISS
>   I love you Gerald.

Bliss and Gerald share a long kiss. Some guests CHEER and the minister looks on in approval.

MUSIC starts playing and people start dancing. Some wedding guests line up to greet the couple.

>   MALE GUEST ONE
>   Beautiful! All the effects of
>   a large wedding, but in a small,
>   private ceremony. Wonderful job
>   you two. I'm proud of you son.

(cont'd)

(cont'd)

The guest hugs the smiling bride.

As the guest hugs and Gerald, Bliss greets another guest.

          BLISS
So good to see you again.

        FEMALE GUEST ONE
I wish some of your family or friends could have made it. Maybe we'll meet some of them during the holidays.

The mature Anglo lady hugs Gerald.

         GERALD
Surely, mother.

An Asian-American lady younger than her hugs Bliss.

        FEMALE GUEST TWO
Congratulations. We're glad you are part of our family.

        MALE GUEST TWO
Thank you for taking him off our hands.

Bliss and Gerald hug the two guests.

         GERALD
See baby, even my step-parents wish I wasn't moving away.

A tanned Hispanic woman approaching Bliss and Gerald overhears his comments.

         GERALD
And they're not the only ones. Treat me right, now Bliss.

(cont'd)

(cont'd)

> FEMALE GUEST THREE
> Treat him bad girl for his
> dogged-out exes. Just kidding.

The female hugs Bliss as if sincere.

> FEMALE GUEST THREE
> You and her look perfect for
> each other you know. I can't
> imagine all the experiences
> love will bring to your lives.

She hugs Gerald as Bliss greets other guests while watching and listening to the female guest talk to Gerald.

> FEMALE GUEST THREE
> I'm so proud of the man you
> have become. Your wife is
> evidence of your achievements.
> Don't lose sight of the love
> you have, and never let her
> think your love for her has
> changed -- unless it has.

She looks at Bliss and smiles, then looks back at G.

> FEMALE GUEST THREE
> Congratulations. The best life
> has for you will be delivered
> through your wife, as long as
> you do those things required
> of you in the husband role.

The female guest kisses Gerald on the cheek and rubs his arm as she walks away.

Gerald is smiling and Bliss looks bothered.

> BLISS
> Should I even ask?

(cont'd)

(cont'd)

                    GERALD
        That was her.

                    BLISS
        Her eyes said it as she
        stood in line. Well, it's
        good to meet the mistress
        ahead of time.

                    GERALD
        I will never put you
        through anything like
        that. You're the only
        woman for me.

INT. AIRPORT TERMINAL - NIGHT

Flight attendants VEMI and JAMES are seen talking to an
airport worker named TY at the ticket counter. The three
walk away from the counter talking.

                    VEMI
        Had I known all this came
        with the job, hell, I would
        have become a flight attendant
        long before I got married,
        kids and a divorce.

                    TY
        Hum. If it wasn't for you
        fliers and your dramatics, us
        ground folk would have nothing
        to keep us going. You all
        bring the excitement - with
        all your shady dealings city to
        city. These are some elaborate
        webs. Keep 'em tight though, or
        hell will break loose if any
        strings unravel it all apart.

(cont'd)

(cont'd)

                    JAMES
Ty, I warn that all the time, but you know you can't tell grown people a thing. I'm just glad I have a wife at home and I'm not looking for more love or money than I've already accepted. Trying to fulfill the needs of the pocket and heart, I say, is the root of most of this wrong stuff we know people do. Staying out of doing wrong myself is the only other job I need.

                    TY
And if I don't quit talking to you suits, I won't be keeping this maintenance job I need. Time for me to go and get my khakis dirty! You all, have a nice flight, and tell your co-workers, mainly Bliss, Tyrone said to keep it on lock and lock it well.

Ty, Vemi and James share a laugh as Ty gathers his duffle bag and jacket.

Ty jogs away as Vemi and James wave good-bye.

Vemi and James begin quickly walking down the corridor, then they veer left.

A few seconds later, Bliss runs down the same corridor and places her hat on her head as she veers left.

INT. AIRPLANE - NIGHT

Bliss boards the plane.

                    BLISS
James! Hello.

                                              (cont'd)

(cont'd)

                    JAMES
Always a pleasure to see you Bliss. And Ty says hello and tighten the lock, keep the lock locked, or something.

                    BLISS
Keep it locked tight. We just ran past each other and he yelled

James opens the cockpit door and Bliss steps in as Vemi passes by and smiles.

                    BLISS
Vemi! Ready for take-off in . . . say three.

                    VEMI
We'll be ready.

                    JAMES
Home, here we come!

Bliss CHUCKLES and sits in the pilot's seat, immediately buckling her seat belt.

James steps outside the cockpit and CLOSES THE DOOR.

Vemi and James make eye contact, and James shakes his head.

INT. COCKPIT - NIGHT

Bliss is flipping switches, touching and analyzing equipment, and jotting notes.

She presses a yellow button.

BEEP is heard.

Bliss resumes flipping switches and jots a few notes.

(cont'd)

(cont'd)

She presses the yellow button again. BUSY TONE is heard.

Bliss SIGHS.

She presses the yellow button again.

BUSY TONE is heard.

                    BLISS
          Okay, what's going on?

She presses the yellow button again.

BUSY TONE.

She presses the yellow button again.

TWO BEEPS.

                    BLISS
         Ready Vemi? Is everyone
         seated for the journey?

                    VEMI
         Pretty much?

                    BLISS
         You stayed out of
         trouble while off work
         didn't you?

                    VEMI
         As far as the proof
         says, and the proof is
         all that matters so I'm
         not trying to leave a
         paper trail.

(cont'd)

                    BLISS
          Gotcha! The flight should be an easy early arrival, so we can all resume living pretty soon. Are our ever so lovely passengers as ready to get home as we are?

                    VEMI
          I wondered that too, but they all are finally seated and now we're ready for you to taxi.

                    BLISS
          Life is beautiful.

INT. AIRPLANE - NIGHT

Passengers are being served beverages and peanuts by TWO OTHER FLIGHT ATTENDANTS and Vemi.

James is standing as though he is securing the plane.

The flight attendant passing out peanuts gives a little boy the last pack, then begins assisting Vemi and the other attendant with beverages.

Vemi leaves the two attendants to finish serving the drinks. James sees Vemi approach him.

                    JAMES
          Everyone seems to be calm today.

                    VEMI
          Not everybody.

(cont'd)

(cont'd)

Vemi grabs James's left hand and pulls on him.

          VEMI
    Come with me.

          JAMES
    Where?

          VEMI
    Where do you think?
    Let's go to the station
    and chat before the
    others make it over here
    and Speed Racer gets us
    home.

          JAMES
    What's up?

          VEMI
    You know what's up.

Vemi and James walk behind a purple curtain.

          JAMES
    You make things so
    obvious.

          VEMI
    People don't pay as much
    attention to things as
    your paranoia makes you
    think they do.

          JAMES
    I'm schizophrenic? Vemi!
    You're as discreet as
    crab lice, as nosey as a
    neighbor, and as loud as
    a tacky outfit too big
    for the anorexic wearing

(cont'd)

(cont'd)

> JAMES (cont'd)
> it. And then you're obvious! Why do you think Bliss won't really get close to you, and I don't tell you my business? Pleasantries on the job are one thing. Friends spend time together outside of work.

> VEMI
> Me and Bliss close, and me and you too! If we wasn't, how could I know your anniversary coming up this month and Bliss just got married this weekend?

> JAMES
> My anniversary is on Halloween, so everyone knows that. And I thought you told me Bliss was married when I first started with here.

> VEMI
> I did and she was.

> JAMES
> So she and Davis have gotten a divorce and we had no idea. When did she start dating her second husband?

(cont'd)

(cont'd)

>VEMI
>Davis was her second, Menard is her first. This new one is named Gerald.

>JAMES
>No! Are you sure? I've never even heard her mention Menard!

>VEMI
>Think about it, do you hear her mention Davis? Did you hear her mention dating Gerald or even having a wedding over the weekend? Miss Bliss smells sweet like honeysuckle, but she's heartless. She has old money plus new money, and she doesn't know when enough of anything is enough.

>JAMES
>Don't be jealous of her because of her money and love life now Vemi.

>VEMI
>I might not have love anymore, but I get money and men at least pretend like they love me, so I'm not jealous of her at all because she has nothing that I don't have already.

(cont'd)

(cont'd)

                    JAMES
I just know that she's not all together like she comes off. Nobody on earth is.

                    VEMI
If she had it all together like she acts like she does, she won't be so secretive 'n shit all the time. I admit I make extra money spending time with men in the cities we fly to, but what is she doing? All she's admitted is being married, but Miss Thing must forget I've been flying with her for five years. She's been married three times since I've been here. Hell, where the other two 'et 'cause she ain't been grieving. I wanna know if she paid somebody or if she killed 'em huhself?

EXT. FREEWAY - DAY CLOSE IN ON INTERIOR OF CHAMPAGNE EXCURSION.

Bliss is riding with Gerald, MENARD and DAVIS.

She is reading a CD jacket and begins listening to the men talk.

The discussion among the men becomes louder.

                                      (cont'd)

(cont'd)

> **BLISS**
> I really don't understand why this topic is even a discussion, especially right now. I'm just making it back into town and I'm ready to go home - and not hear stuff like this.

> **DRIVER**
> What?

> **GERALD**
> Menard's right. You are the reason for all this Bliss.

> **DAVIS**
> Nah G, the both of ya'll is wrong. We chose to be a part of her bull, so we can't just put all the blame over on Bliss like that.

Bliss turns in her seat and looks at each of the three men, smirks, and looks at the Davis and Gerald again.

> **BLISS**
> Davis, your attempt to stick up for me while sticking me up was rather noble. However, might I remind you all, none of you were forced into this, and none are forced to stay in it.

Bliss looks around and points at the men.

(cont'd)

(cont'd)

>   BLISS
>   Do whatever you feel you
>   have to do; because, you
>   sure know, I do whatever
>   I think I should so I
>   will be okay no matter
>   what could happen with
>   me and you three.

Bliss grabs a CD and pushes it in the player with her thumb.

She then twirls a lock of her hair and looks out the window.

Menard and Gerald look angered.

Davis looks as though he likes what Bliss had said.

>   MENARD
>   You are a piece of work,
>   you know that, Bliss?

>   GERALD
>   Man, I don't see how you
>   two even let her bring
>   me into this. I thought
>   I was going home to be
>   with my beautiful wife!
>   What I found is that I
>   was lured into the belly
>   of the beast!

>   BLISS
>   So I'm a beast now?

Davis reaches his hands around the passenger seat's head rest. He begins massaging Bliss's shoulders.

Gerald looks disgusted. Menard glances over.

(cont'd)

(cont'd)

                    GERALD
You weren't honest with me Bliss! This was supposed to be our beginning! You didn't lay everything on the line! You didn't give me the chance you gave them to walk away! Is it because I'm not Black?

                    BLISS
I thought race was a non-issue with us G.

Davis SIGHS.

                    DAVIS
Reverse racism . . . reciprocity . . . alpha to omega!

                    GERALD
You racist prick!

                    DAVIS
We have plenty of friends of who tan, buddy. Advice: Fresh arrivals with short stays find speedy departures more comfortable.

Menard looks angrier than he already was.

Davis looks smug.

Gerald looks puzzled.

Bliss looks unphased.

(cont'd)

(cont'd)

                    MENARD
          Listen to this shit!
          Davis, buddy, did you
          forget? You are number
          two and now there's a
          number three. Bliss said
          we would know about any
          newbies long before they
          were in this to stay. We
          didn't know about him
          and he didn't know about
          us.

Davis continues massaging Bliss shoulders, frequently rubbing her shoulders and upper arms.

                    MENARD
          A man and a woman are
          only as much a man or a
          woman as his or her
          ability to keep the
          promises made. We had an
          agreement that Bliss
          broke! And if anybody
          should be being petted
          with massages and
          supportive words, it
          should be us, not Bliss!

Bliss tries to turn around in her seat, but Davis grips her arms, preventing her mobility.

Davis leans forward and whispers to Bliss.

                    DAVIS
          Keep still and stay quiet.

Davis resumes massaging Bliss.

Bliss begins to relax and get comfortable.

                                          (cont'd)

(cont'd)

> MENARD
> Now G, this is that psycho zone I was telling you about. We got a raw deal! I'm ready to leave this all behind me and return to the real world. I'll rather be out there struggling and living the way I want to live than to be well off and living out a task list written by somebody else. But number two is just happy to step-and-fetch and be a part of this . . . mess she's making.

> DAVIS
> Well, being a man of my word, I'll stay in this until death takes me out of it. We all knew what to expect before we got to this point. Even you, G, knew this was an unusual and risky endeavor before you took part in the ceremony.

> MENARD
> True, it's not as pain-free as we thought, but it is more rewarding than we were promised.

Bliss smiled a pompous smile.

(cont'd)

                MENARD
For the rest of my life, I'll keep enjoying myself in this, and letting Bliss know when I have a problem and what the problem is with. After that, I'll just have to be cool with whatever and her too, truth be told.

                DAVIS
I'm with Bliss and down for whatever regardless. We're not in this by force. Go if you're not happy. Two of three would love to be the one and only.

                GERALD
More power to you, but that's what I came for. That's where I was led to believe I'll be automatically.

                MENARD
That's where I've been. If you ever attain it D, and I don't think you will while I'm alive cause I'm in the number one spot, you won't be able to hold it for long.

(cont'd)

(cont'd)

DAVIS
Nonetheless, I bet I'll be the last one in it, man. And hey, let a brother know if you need help packing. I have luggage I can let you have to pack up the extra stuff you got under Bliss's roof.

MENARD
(to Gerald)
Who is this nigga?

GERALD
That's what I was gonna ask?

DAVIS
Nah podna, that's a question you better never ask?

GERALD
What?

BLISS
Men, men, please! And you all talk about women being at each other's throats. The testosterone level is working my nerves, but damn you're making me horny! If you three could be friends long enough, we could really enjoy all 50,000 square feet at home.

(cont'd)

(cont'd)

Menard looks disgusted.

Davis looks pleased.

Gerald looks puzzled.

> BLISS
> Will you take the exit to Kimera's for me M? If she's there, I'll have her to bring me home in about an hour.

> GERALD
> It would really be good, Bliss, if you would come home so we can iron things out.

> BLISS
> What is the confusion G?

> GERALD
> You weren't honest with me - with none of us.

> BLISS
> I apologize, and the truth is common now.

> MENARD
> That doesn't make it right.

> BLISS
> Do you forgive me Menard?

> MENARD
> I do, but I want you to stop doing this to me.

(cont'd)

(cont'd)

> **BLISS**
> What is done cannot be undone, but I promise you that I will not compound our problems. I won't accept a fourth husband.

> **GERALD**
> There's no way you're serious about even having considered a fourth!

> **DAVIS**
> When have I not been enough for you? You wouldn't want me to do you like this.

> **BLISS**
> No I wouldn't, and you are enough for me.

> **GERALD**
> Then why did I walk away from my family to marry you and come here?

> **BLISS**
> Maybe to prove or disprove something, but also because we have love.

> **GERALD**
> And you love Menard and Davis too?

(cont'd)

(cont'd)

> BLISS
> Even more than I love you. . . . Anything nurtured grows in time.

Menard smiles and exits the freeway.

INT. KIMERA'S HOUSE - DAY

KIMERA is wiping down a kitchen counter as she frequently glances at Bliss.

> KIMERA
> Your timing is perfect.

> BLISS
> You just got settled well?

> KIMERA
> Funchess dropped by for a quick dinner before going home. He left about 30 minutes ago.

Kimera walks to the dining room table and removes dirty dishes.

> BLISS
> How long has it been for you two?

Kimera returns to the kitchen saying:

> KIMERA
> Together, five years; last time we had sex, two weeks; and years waiting for him to leave his wife, six.

The ladies LAUGH LOUDLY.

(cont'd)

(cont'd)

> **BLISS**
> But girl, you know married men making mistresses are more prone to stay at home than turn the knob and never touch it again.

> **KIMERA**
> As hard as it is for me to accept, I'm realizing that I, unfortunately, won't be one of the women to disprove that.

Kimera begins washing the collected dishes by hand.

> **BLISS**
> I can relate. I wish I could disprove the notion that you can't have your cake and eat it too. I thought the cake, with the icing, was all about consumption. Too much cake is too much weight.

> **KIMERA**
> I like the cake.

> **BLISS**
> Me too, but it still doesn't taste the way I want it too. It's good, don't get me wrong, but it's beginning to go bad.

> **KIMERA**
> Bad? How?

(cont'd)

(cont'd)

                    BLISS
Which version do you want to hear: quick or long?

                    KIMERA
Quickies with long ones are so refreshing, but since this is you and we're having a conversation about a story, I'll drop the quickie from my mind and stick with the image of a long one laid before me.

                    BLISS
You're so freaky minded.

                    KIMERA
My libido does that to my brain sometimes. I'm sorry girl. Tell me the long story. No. I don't have a lot of dishes to wash, so quick is better.

Dishes CLACK.

                    BLISS
Well, you know I was with Menard since he interviewed me for the newspaper article. You were with me two years later when I met Davis and his band. I told you about meeting Gerald when he painted me at a patio café in New York.

(cont'd)

(cont'd)

                KIMERA
I'm with you.

                BLISS
I accepted proposals from them all, got married to them, and now they live with me and I don't know what is going to happen next. I just know something bad is going to happen because it already is starting - and Gerald has only been at my husband for four days and at the house with Menard and Davis for two days.

                KIMERA
I think you lost me.

                BLISS
Listen to me Kimera.

                              DISSOLVE

FLASHBACK

INT. CHURCH WEDDING - DAY

Images of Menard and Bliss's wedding before a large crowd and being broadcast on various television stations are seen as Bliss's continuing monologue is now a voice-over.

                BLISS (V.O.)
Menard moved in with me when we got married. To him, he moved into my home and we live in Missouri.

                              DISSOLVE

                                  (cont'd)

(cont'd)

EXT. UNDERWATER - DAY

Two scuba divers come face-to-face and later one nods the head and the two "kiss" as Bliss's continuing monologue is now a voice-over.

> BLISS (V.O.)
> When Davis asked me to marry him, it just so happened to be on the same day Menard did. I said yes to him too. He thinks he moved in with me and we live in Louisiana.

END FLASHBACK
     DISSOLVE

INT. KIMERA'S HOUSE - DAY

Kimera is washing dishes and RUNNING WATER to rinse them. Bliss is leaning against the kitchen doorway CLICKING AND TAPPING her feet with her arms folded.

> BLISS
> I married Gerald a few days ago, and Tennessee is where he knows we are. Gerald is another story in himself. He's already caused a bit of turbulence. I promised Menard today there wouldn't be a fourth. Plus, the Mississippi part of the place is all I have left that's solely mine, so marrying another man is far from desired right now. I need a place of refuge.

(cont'd)

(cont'd)

Kimera finishes the dishes and is RUNNING WATER, washing the sink before cleaning the dishrag and hanging it to dry.

                  KIMERA
How can we be best friends and you not trust me with all those wild details until now?

                  BLISS
Girl, you don't even trust an "I love you" from your dad.

Kimera washes her hands, RIPS a piece of perforated paper towel from the roll and dries her hands.

                  KIMERA
I'm just saying girl. You never let me know that's what was really going on with you and all of that ya'll over there. I gotta commend you though for hiding all that drama because the media would love it, especially these nuts around here. I'll lie for ya girl, but not to ya. Shoot, you aught to show your podna love and break me off one of those specimen!

Kimera takes a seat next to Bliss.

                  BLISS
That is nasty girl. Don't get cut.

                                            (cont'd)

(cont'd)

KIMERA
Woman, you have three men living with you that you have sex with, and you say I'm nasty because I ask for sex with just one of them.

BLISS
I said you're nasty because I think it's nasty to sleep with men who have sex with your friends and family. Can you take me home when you come to a stopping point because I told the three stooges I'll be home in about an hour, but I also need to stop by Doc's office real quick.

KIMERA
I can do it with no problem.

EXT. MOUNTAINOUS FREEWAY. BLACK ALTIMA - DAY

Bliss is riding with Kimera and listening to "Still Down" by Jon B and Tupac play.

KIMERA
Go white boy. Speaking of that, I can't wait to meet Gerald. I have to see what European can turn your head. I already know Menard and Davis are Puerto Rican and African deities.

(cont'd)

(cont'd)

The women nod their heads and smile.

> KIMERA
> Anyway, and don't complain about how good you have it, and don't worry about losing anything. Lady, who do you know that lives the life you live anyway? Nobody! I ain't never even heard of anybody doing the stuff I know you do.

Bliss SIGHS.

> KIMERA
> Reality isn't always what's seen. Sometimes, things
> we think will bring us joy can only bring us more pain. I know about that. I also know that sometimes we can be sucked into the pain. Don't get sucked in Bliss. You're better than that.

> BLISS
> It's like I can feel Earth planting mines along my course. I know feeding selfish pleasures and breaking laws aren't right, but love changes and so does its rules if you're playing for the staying.

(cont'd)

(cont'd)

                    KIMERA
          That's right. So through
          all eight phases of
          love, we need to show
          we're fit to survive.
          Baby, if it's good for
          you and good to you,
          stay in until you're
          taken out. Or until you
          expose those pupils and
          sniff some java.

Kimera's tires SCREECH as she abruptly stops at the yellow light.

A passing car's HORNBLOWS.

                    BLISS
          Your driving is going to
          kill me one day if I
          keep riding with you.

                    KIMERA
          Back to the subject.

INT. GROCERY STORE - DAY

Kimera is cruising the isle shopping while Bliss pushes the cart.

                    BLISS
          Love is not love if it
          changes the moment
          change becomes feasibly
          optional.

                    KIMERA
          What do you think you
          love about your life?

Bliss picks up cookies then puts them back.

(cont'd)

(cont'd)

                    BLISS
Everything, on the surface. Deep down, though, where my fire really lives, sometimes I feel like I only love me. But most times, I feel like I shouldn't love because I'm prone to lose everything.

                    KIMERA
That's fear talking. What is there that can really rock your world apart?

INT. HOSPITAL - DAY

Bliss is dressed in a gown and talking with a doctor.

DOC hands bliss a clipboard.

                    BLISS
See Doc, just as promised, I came to see you the first moment I had after making it back into town.

                    DOC
Ready for ascension?

                    BLISS
Ready for elation!

                    DOC
Flip the clipboard over and read my finding.

Bliss turns the clipboard face-up and begins to cry.

                                    (cont'd)

(cont'd)

                    DOC
Beautiful! I love to see tears of joy.

                    BLISS
There's nothing good about this right now.

                    DOC
Everything's good about this. This is going to you're your life better. It's okay Bliss. You're a married woman.

                    BLISS
Doc, marriage does not equate to ease.

                    DOC
But Bliss, it's not like you're getting younger or you'll miss the money lost due to maternity leave.

Doc grabs his clipboard and rubs Bliss's back in an effort to be compassionate and comfort her.

                    DOC
Your husband will be happy to hear that he'll soon be a father.

                    BLISS
Husband! Father! Not right now, but it is right now! What have I gotten us into?

                    DOCTOR
It's going to be alright. Everything will work out.

                                  (cont'd)

(cont'd)

                    BLISS
          I don't know.

Bliss buries her face in her hands and wails.

                    DOC
          What don't you know?

                    BLISS
          I don't know what to do.
          I have no idea what I
          can do to make this not
          escalate the problems at
          home already.

                    DOC
          I recommend going home
          in good spirits, and
          telling him when the
          time is right. You have
          a few weeks before he
          figures it out himself.
          Congratulations.

FADE OUT

FADE IN

INT. KIMERA'S CAR - DAY

Kimera is driving. Bliss is hanging up the telephone.

                    BLISS
          Finally, no calls to
          immediately return.

                    KIMERA
          Hopefully it'll stay
          that way for a minute.
          The less stress you
          have, the better the
          next year will be.

                                (cont'd)

(cont'd)

           BLISS
You're always so optimistic.

           KIMERA
Not about everything.

           BLISS
About most things though, especially when things look so bleak.

           KIMERA
Girl, since we've become friends, my life has improved greatly, and I want to replenish your happiness any time I can because you've given me so much of it.

           BLISS
That's sweet.

           KIMERA
That's the truth. Since we became friends, I've met so many other friends who are real friends too. I ain't never had real friends before. I'm glad we're friends, and I won't ever leave your side.

           BLISS
Ooh, don't talk like that. You sound like you're going to die or something. Let's change the subject.

(cont'd)

(cont'd)

                    KIMERA
I'm gonna be fine girl.

EXT. AERIAL VIEW OF BLISS'S PROPERTY - DAY

A man is riding a LAWNMOWER cutting the grass on the side lawn.

Menard is trimming hedges on the front lawn at the driveway's curve nearest the house.

The front door CHIMES as it is opened from the inside.

Menard looks up and stops working.

                    MENARD
Yes?

Gerald steps out.

                    GERALD
Have a minute?

                    MENARD
For what?

                    GERALD
I'm just trying to get an understanding man. I didn't come for no trouble - bringing or giving.

                    MENARD
Talk to Bliss man. I got problems of my own that I'm dealing with - my own understanding to get.

(cont'd)

(cont'd)

> GERALD
> I feel like I was lured into a project. We all were.

> MENARD
> You and Davis, yeah. Me, no, not at all.

Menard CRANKS the trimmer and resumes trimming a hedge.

Gerald shakes his head, goes into the house, and the DOOR SHUTS.

INT. BLISS'S HOME - DAY

Hallway desk PHONE RINGS.

Davis is in the kitchen preparing dinner.

Gerald is walking down the hallway and answers the telephone.

> GERALD
> Gerald speaking.

> CALLER (O.S.)
> This is your mother. How's everything? You've really been on my mind a lot today

> GERALD
> We're still transitioning. How's everyone back home?

> GERALD'S MOTHER (O.S.)
> Happy for you and worried about you.

(cont'd)

                  GERALD
There's no need to worry. I'll be fine.

INT. HOME OF GERALD'S MOTHER - DAY

               GERALD'S MOTHER
What are you eating? I don't know how a woman with her schedule can maintain a home to perfection with such limited time on her hands.

              GERALD (O.S.)
Dinner is cooking now mother and it smells great.

               GERALD'S MOTHER
Are you cooking?

INT. BLISS'S HOME - DAY

                  GERALD
No. I don't have to worry about cooking. Her home management methods are definitely unlike any I've ever seen. I'm passing time by doing a few loads of clothes.

           GERALD'S MOTHER (O.S.)
Umph. You know you can always come home within the next month if you need to, and everything can be put behind you.

                  GERALD
Let me talk to you later mother.

(cont'd)

(cont'd)

                GERALD'S MOTHER (O.S.)
          We're not racist you
          know.

                GERALD
          I love you all too.
          Goodbye.

Gerald hangs up the phone.

                GERALD
          Family! If it ain't one
          thing, it's something
          else.

INT. VEMI'S HOME - DAY

Vemi is on the telephone with two friends on three-way.

Vemi LOUDLY LAUGHS and does a KNEE SLAP.

                VEMI
          You better believe it.
          Don't be confused honey,
          nothing gets past the
          Misses. I am pure oil.
          You can't slick the
          slickest. So I put
          somebody on it, one of
          my own hook-ups.

                FRIEND ONE
          That's a whole 'nother
          level if you're talking
          PI.

                VEMI
          It's all about the
          facts.

(cont'd)

(cont'd)

                FRIEND TWO
       What you call fact,
       somebody else will call
       fiction. A fact ain't
       nothing but a documented
       perspective generally
       accepted by some
       percentage of the
       people.

                VEMI
       Ah, whatever. I'm
       supposed to meet my guy
       toNIGHT Wanna go with
       me. We can catch a movie
       after we eat.

      FRIEND ONE/FRIEND TWO
       Free?

                VEMI
       For ya'll but not for
       me.

                FRIEND TWO
       I'm in!

                FRIEND ONE
       Me three!

INT. BLISS'S HOME - DAY

Gerald walks into the laundry room.

Davis is still preparing dinner in the kitchen.

Gerald begins loading a basket full of jeans in the dryer.

He throws in a dryer sheet before SLAMMING DRYER DOOR, setting the timer for 45 minutes, and starting the machine.

                                          (cont'd)

(cont'd)

The front door CHIMES as it is opened by Menard for Bliss to enter first.

Menard closes the door once he is inside the house.

Gerald and Davis come into the greeting room where Bliss and Menard stand talking.

              MENARD
Would you want me to do this?

              BLISS
You have.

              MENARD
You're the only wife I've ever had.

              BLISS
Not if I'm not the only woman you've had sex with.

              DAVIS
That's a bit extreme. You know this is a foul situation Bliss. What about you having this motto of not expecting any more of anyone than what you can give them of you?

              GERALD
So we all hear the same things huh? How fucking special is that shit?

              BLISS
I'm the same woman aren't I, and you do want to know the truth right?

                              (cont'd)

(cont'd)

                  MENARD
As if total truth is what you've been giving us Bliss. I really don't have to take this.

                  DAVIS
You keep saying that. Am I the only one without extra ass?

                  BLISS
I can't take this conversation anymore. I'll be back. I need to bathe and think about things. Davis, I'll be down for dinner in about 45 minutes if that's not too late.

                  DAVIS
That's fine baby, but you owe us a talk at dinner. The total truth talk takes place tonight with all four of us present and calm.

                  MENARD
That's right.

                  BLISS
See you all shortly. Menard, Gerald, Davis, I apologize.

Bliss walks out of the room.

The men look across the room at each other.

Davis pulls the towel from his shoulder and walks back into the kitchen.

                            (cont'd)

(cont'd)

                    GERALD
          I guess I'll dust until
          our jeans dry.

Gerald walks out of the sunroom.

Menard sits at the piano, pulls a moist towelette and cleans his hands. He puts the used towelette into a small golden tray next to the dispenser, then begins playing an original mellow tune on the piano.

The PHONE RINGS.

Menard stops playing the piano and answers the phone.

                    MENARD
          This is Menard.

                    KIMERA
          Hey Menard! May I speak
          with Bliss please?

                    MENARD
          Didn't she just leave
          from being with you?
          Hold on.

                    KIMERA
          Some folks are just
          trifling.

                    MENARD
          And others are so
          uncouth. One moment
          please.

INT. RESTAURANT - NIGHT

Vemi is with two women who leave when a man comes and sits at the table with her.

                    VEMI
          Thanks. Any luck on
          those three?

                              (cont'd)

(cont'd)

> MAN
> Of course I do. She was born Bliss Serenity Hope in Brooklyn. She's married to Menard LeRoy Datiz.

> VEMI
> No other husbands?

> MAN
> No.

INT. BLISS'S STUDY - NIGHT

Bliss is wearing a white dress and has her hair up.

She grabs the yellow book titled "Life IS Beautiful by Mylia Jaza" from the shelf.

Bliss sits on the desktop.

She looks at the cover, glances at the back, then opens it and reads a poem aloud.

> BLISS
> Musings/Nothing is absolute./Life is sketched by you./Exude excellence infinitely./Moving mountains many times means making rocks crumble./Aspirations never materialize when they are only visualized. /Inferiority is a complex: Superiority is a consciousness./Some people work to fool themselves daily in order to maintain satisfaction.

(cont'd)

(cont'd)

The intercom BUZZES.

Bliss presses the button on the wall.

> BLISS
> I'm on my way down.

> DAVIS
> Sounds good.

Bliss releases the intercom button. She flips the pages of the yellow book of poetry, then grabs the white book of the same title from the shelf.

> BLISS
> Here goes.

Bliss walks out of the study with the books in her left hand.

EXT. MOVIE THEATRE - NIGHT

Kimera and Vemi notice eachother as they walk through flanking doors of the theatre.

> VEMI
> Hello.

> KIMERA
> Hi.

Kimera's and Vemi's facial expressions were of friendly familiarity.

The two girls with Vemi at the restaurant get in line to order popcorn.

Kimera is talking with FUNCHESS.

> FUNCHESS
> Be sure to tell Bliss congratulations. Want some nachos and a pop?

(cont'd)

(cont'd)

                KIMERA
What are you getting for you?

               FUNCHESS
I'm got my drink in my pocket. I'll get a hot dog and some popcorn probably.

                KIMERA
I don't know what I want yet. I need to wash my hands first though.

               FUNCHESS
Sweetheart, I really have to dip to the restroom like crazy. Here's the money. Order me a hot dog with everything, some popcorn, and a large pop. Get whatever you want too. Okay?

                KIMERA
Alright. Hurry up though, and wash your hands.

Kimera gets in a line next to the line Vemi and her friends are in.

Vemi approaches Kimera.

                 VEMI
You're Bliss's friend aren't you?

                KIMERA
Who? Who are you?

(cont'd)

(cont'd)

                    VEMI
I'm Vemi. I'm a flight attendant with The Airline, and I work with Bliss.

                    KIMERA
I thought I'd seen you somewhere.

                    VEMI
You looked familiar too, and when I heard your husband say congratulate her for him, that's when I knew where I knew you from.

                    KIMERA
Not trying to be mean, but eavesdropping is not impressive.

                    VEMI
My fault. I wasn't trying to be nosey, but I just overheard him say that. Bliss and I are real cool.

                    KIMERA
Okay. Your friends are waiting for you.

Vemi returns to the line with her friends.

Funchess approaches, turns away, and goes back into the restroom.

Kimera laughs and moves forward in line.

INT. BLISS'S FAMILY DINING ROOM - NIGHT

(cont'd)

(cont'd)

Gerald, Menard and Davis are sitting at the round dining room table.

Menard re-arranges the fresh flower centerpiece, then sits.

Bliss pours their tea and brings their plates to them.

She sets her plate on the table, sits and pours herself tea.

Menard stands.

> MENARD
> Bliss, can we trust you?
> Will you . . .

>> DISSOLVE

FLASHBACK

EXT. TRACK FIELD - DAY

Bliss jogs the track and picks up her pace.

COACH is on the sideline timing her.

Bliss nears the finish line.

As she crosses and stops running, she begins to hyperventilate.

> COACH
> We have to work on
> controlling your
> breathing and pacing.

Bliss is bent over and breathing heavy.

She nods her head.

END FLASHBACK
    DISSOLVE

(cont'd)

(cont'd)

INT. BLISS'S FAMILY DINING ROOM - NIGHT

Menard sits.

              MENARD
        Bliss, can you?

              BLISS
        Yes Menard, please sit
        down. Let's say grace
        and enjoy a peaceful
        dinner. Then, we can
        think and talk
        rationally.

              GERALD
        So far, that's the
        truth.

Bliss looks at Davis.

              DAVIS
        Everybody bow your
        heads, close your eyes,
        and you're your hearts.
        Yahweh, thank you for
        being, thank you for
        Yeshua and your Holy
        Spirit, and thank you
        for this healthy and
        delicious meal we are
        able to enjoy. Selah.
        Amen.

              GERALD
        You're a Black Jew?

              DAVIS
        Bliss and I are Hebrew
        Israelites, descendants
        from the tribes of
        Benjamin and Judah. We
        were born chosen.

                            (cont'd)

(cont'd)

>   GERALD
>   I'm Christian. Menard,
>   you're Catholic right?
>
>   MENARD
>   I'll give you that one
>   G. Yeah.
>
>   BLISS
>   Everything tastes superb
>   Davis.
>
>   DAVIS
>   It was hard today I'm
>   glad you like it.
>
>   BLISS
>   I can taste the passion
>   you cooked with - hoping
>   it ain't no voodoo. Do
>   forgive me Davis. I love
>   you so much.
>
>   MENARD
>   Bliss!

Menard and Gerald turn red.

>   BLISS
>   Menard, I love you. You
>   too Gerald.
>
>   GERALD
>   I'm going to the
>   bathroom.

INT. BLISS'S DINING BATHROOM - NIGHT

The DOOR SHUTS and Gerald kneels at the door with his hands on the knob.

(cont'd)

(cont'd)

                    GERALD
God, how did I end up in this? I'm nothing like my family, but I get burned like my family said I would. I don't know what to do. None of us know what to do. Take care of us. Work this mess out for each of us. Amen.

Gerald gets off his knees.

He opens the door and the DOOR SHUTS after he leaves the bathroom.

INT. BLISS'S FAMILY DINING ROOM - NIGHT

Bliss, Menard and Davis are eating, drinking and talking.

Gerald looks closely at each of them as he approaches the table and sits back in his chair.

                    DAVIS
You alright?

                    GERALD
I will be.

                    MENARD
It can get a little hot and lot thick around here sometimes. You sure you can hang?

                    BLISS
He hangs fine, Menard, leave him alone.

(cont'd)

(cont'd)

                    GERALD
I can talk for myself Bliss. Get off my back Menard.

                    MENARD
I'll never get on your back podna. I ain't got no reason to be behind you. I'm trying to not kick your ass.

                    GERALD
I threaten you.

                    MENARD
You wish.

                    DAVIS
You act like he does.

                    BLISS
Peace, please. We were headed down a good path here. Don't ruin the mood.

                    GERALD
All of this is some crazy shit.

Gerald begins eating.

Menard pours himself some tea.

Bliss SIGHS.

Davis looks around the table.
    DISSOLVE

<u>FLASHBACK</u>

INT. DAVIS'S ROOM AT BLISS'S HOUSE - DAY

(cont'd)

                    DAVIS
          I promise.

Bliss and Davis hug.

                    BLISS
          I don't want to lose
          you. Don't let anything
          get between us, ever.
          You are my lifeline. You
          always have been. I love
          you Davis Comas.

Bliss and Davis kiss.

END FLASHBACK
    DISSOLVE

INT. BLISS'S FAMILY DINING ROOM - NIGHT

Bliss is standing and holding a glass of champagne.

                    BLISS
          A toast to friendship
          and love for eternity.

The men hesitantly stand and toast.

All four drink and sit.

They resume eating and talking.

                    DAVIS
          Now is a good time to
          completely clear the
          air.

                    BLISS
          I think so too. Let's
          try not to scream okay
          guys.

(cont'd)

(cont'd)

>   GERALD
> This isn't what I want.
>
>   BLISS
> Do you want to leave?
>
>   GERALD
> Had I known about them before we got married, we wouldn't have gotten married. I feel like I don't even know you - that you're not the woman I met and married. I want children and a life with you, just you and me and our kids.
>
>   BLISS
> I told you that I didn't want bi-racial children because I didn't want to further complicate my children's lives.
>
>   MENARD
> You said what? I'm bi-racial. I'm half Puerto Rican and half African American.
>
>   DAVIS
> I'm Black, 100% African American. I ain't got no problems mating.

Gerald and Menard look angrily at Davis and Bliss's grinning.

>   GERALD
> That's so racist Bliss. How could you love me, yet not want to have children with me.

(cont'd)

(cont'd)

>>BLISS
>>Is ejaculatory fluid all you have to offer me?

>>GERALD
>>No. I have plenty of love to give. But looking at your lifestyle here, no amount I alone possess will be enough for you.

>>BLISS
>>I need companionship and love, support and commitment.

>>MENARD
>>We need those things too. But what kind of commitment are you making with us tonight? We support you and we're loving companions, and we shouldn't have to go through this.

>>DAVIS
>>Pick one, send two steppin'.

>>BLISS
>>It's not that simple.

Gerald begins THROAT CLEARING.

>>GERALD
>>If you pulled all this off, anything should be simple to you.

(cont'd)

              MENARD
     No kidding.

              DAVIS
     Who do you love most?

              BLISS
     Myself.

Bliss eats a forkful of vegetables.

              GERALD
     Out of us three, who do
     you love most?

              BLISS
     That should be of least
     concern to you. There
     are larger problems
     before us. Nonetheless,
     I love you equally.

              MENARD
     You're a liar. That's
     impossible.

Menard eats a piece of meat.

              BLISS
     You're a liar if you
     really want us to
     believe that it's
     impossible. You've even
     told me that you never
     thought you'd love
     anyone the way you first
     loved, until you met me.

Menard stops eating.

(cont'd)

(cont'd)

> MENARD
> That's different because I love one love at a time.

> BLISS
> I fell in love with you all at different times.

> GERALD
> How could that happen if you love any of us. What about monogamy? Isn't this illegal anyway?

> BLISS
> Please baby.

INT. DEPARTMENT STORE - DAY

Bliss, Gerald, Menard and Davis are in the men's section looking at shirts.

> GERALD
> How long do you think we'll play lawnboy, maid and cook for you? I can get this whole mess of mine annulled, and never look back.

Bliss strolls to a nearby chair, sits in it, and crosses her arms.

> BLISS
> So, you don't love me and never have?

> GERALD
> That's not what I said.

(cont'd)

(cont'd)

              BLISS
But is that what you feel?

              GERALD
You know I love you Bliss. Hell, even Menard and Davis know I love you.

Menard and Davis look up, and at each other.

              MENARD
But Bliss, it's not like either of these clowns love you like I do.

Menard and Bliss look at each other.

Bliss gets up and walks to the row across from the men.

              MENARD
Not many men would stay faithful to you through something like this.

              BLISS
Are you practicing monogamy with me?

Davis is watching Bliss's reactions closely as he moves to the isle behind Bliss and looks at shirts.

Menard is staring at Bliss, and he looks hurt.

              MENARD
You already know the answer.

              BLISS
Give me confirmation. Who all are you doin'?

(cont'd)

(cont'd)

>   MENARD
>   Only you, and by choice
>   - often I wonder why.
>
>   BLISS
>   Then why stay with me?

Bliss looks sad and slightly bows her head.

>   MENARD
>   You're my wife, till
>   death do us apart, and
>   my one and only.
>
>   GERALD
>   She said that to all us
>   man, so that means
>   nothing right now.

Bliss looks up, but still seems sad.

>   BLISS
>   I did mean what I said.
>   I plan to never divorce
>   either of you. You'll
>   have to leave me for us
>   to be apart.

Davis is watching Bliss closely.

Gerald goes to the isle Bliss is on and begins shopping.

>   DAVIS
>   And you can just let go
>   that quick?
>
>   BLISS
>   I can.

Davis was stunned. He quickly erased the emotion from his face.

(cont'd)

(cont'd)

                    DAVIS
Where's the love in that? If it goes so quickly, especially after coming so slowly, is it even love?

                    BLISS
I'll tell you what love is. Love is having a baby when you don't know who its father is.

                    MENARD
That's not love, that's living out a fuck-up.

There is SILENCE.

                    BLISS
That's a love of life despite the circumstances you face.

                    GERALD
Not if you're not living wisely by learning from the lesson.

                    DAVIS
Wait. Bliss. Are you pregnant?

                    MENARD
This is a scenario we're discussing, not reality.

                    DAVIS
Bliss? Are you pregnant?

Bliss takes a deep breath.

(cont'd)

(cont'd)

EXT. MALL PARKING LOT - DAY

All three men anxiously glance at Bliss as they walk with bags in their hands toward their SUV in view.

                BLISS
I'm not sure.

                GERALD
What do you mean?

                BLISS
I want a second opinion.

                MENARD
Go see Doc.

                BLISS
I already did.

                MENARD
When was this? Before
your last flight out?

                BLISS
Yes, and after I
returned today

                DAVIS
That was the thing to
think about during your
bath, huh?

                BLISS
It was.

                GERALD
I can't believe this. I
know we always used a
condom, but we had an
accident weeks ago.

Menard unlocks the Excursion and opens for the door for Bliss.

                                  (cont'd)

(cont'd)

              MENARD
I don't want to hear that! How could you do this Bliss?

              BLISS
I don't want to get hurt and I don't want to hurt anybody.

Bliss gets into the SUV and Menard closes her door. Gerald laughs out loud. All three men get into the Excursion with Bliss.

              GERALD
How can you say that and do all this? You're hurting us and you by being so afraid to get attached.

              BLISS
I do get attached, but I'm afraid that I will lose love, so I want to love every time love gives me a chance.

Menard begins driving.

              GERALD
That makes no sense. You want to not turn anyone down because you think you'll eventually get dumped by everyone.

              BLISS
No. I turn plenty of people down, but when there is a man that I know loves me and enables me to love him, I love him and let him love me.

                              (cont'd)

(cont'd)

                    MENARD
What extinguishes such fires Bliss? So when does it stop Bliss?

                    BLISS
Today, like I said earlier.

                    DAVIS
Who do you think is the father?

                    BLISS
Honestly, I don't know.

All three men SIGH.

                    MENARD
That's a shame.

                    GERALD
At least now I actually have a chance to get something good from you if the baby is mine.

                    BLISS
You know Gerald, you can leave at any time if I so disgust you. I will not be mistreated, especially not in my own house. I will even pay your moving expenses should you decide to leave.

Davis picks up the CD case and flips through the first few pages of music.

                                                      (cont'd)

(cont'd)

                    DAVIS
        I told ya I got the
        luggage man, and can
        arrange a flight for ya.

                    GERALD
        Why disrespect if you
        don't want to be
        disrespected.

Bliss holds out her left hand toward Davis.

                    DAVIS
        I'm gone find something.

Bliss looks around for a quick second, and keeps her left had held out toward Davis.

Davis gives her the CD case.

                    BLISS
        Thank you.

Bliss begins slowly looking through the CDs.

                    DAVIS
        What are we gonna do
        about this new situation
        we're all in now?

Bliss turns up the right corner of her mouth in disgust.

                    BLISS
        I've already cried
        enough for us all, and
        it changed nothing. Not
        a damn thing. I believe
        reading these books will
        make me feel better, and
        hopefully, inspire some
        new thoughts in this
        head of mine.

                                                (cont'd)

(cont'd)

                    MENARD
          Nobody's told a story as jacked up as ours, so I doubt if there's something you'll run across that'll suddenly make you change.

                    DAVIS
          Anyone can change, it just takes a while for the change to settle in and get noticed.

                    BLISS
          And anything can change. Mutation is a natural thing, a part of the survival process that all life undergoes.

                    MENARD
          Change is still needed over this way. Although so much already has changed, it hasn't necessarily changed for the better.

FADE OUT

FADE IN

EXT. CITY PARK CARNIVAL. BUMPER CARS - DAY

Bliss and Gerald are in line to ride bumper cars.

Bliss is looking around and, although far away, happens to notice that Vemi is at the carnival.

Bliss looks like she is happy to see Vemi.

                                              (cont'd)

(cont'd)

EXT. CITY PARK CARNIVAL. FERRIS WHEEL - DAY

Vemi never sees Bliss.

Vemi is sitting on a bench with the Man who investigated Bliss for Vemi earlier.

> **VEMI**
> Now, this is the husband that you told me about before right.

> **MAN**
> Right.

> **VEMI**
> The first one? The only one that's actually documented.

> **MAN**
> That's him.

Man gives Vemi a manilla envelope. She opens the envelope and pulls out five different photos of Menard at Bliss's house.

> **VEMI**
> These are excellent shots. You did these?

> **MAN**
> Yeap, parked on the road to her house. I stayed in the car and used a mega zoom camera.

Davis and Menard are walking toward Bliss and Gerald, and are about to pass the bench where Vemi and Man sit.

Vemi looks up and watches them as the get closer.

(cont'd)

(cont'd)

> VEMI
> Do you see this?

Vemi and Man both look at Menard and then look at each other.

> MAN
> Like I told you, life always takes care of itself. You just have to sit back more and enjoy what's delivered to your door.

Vemi looks back at the photos, then looks back up at Menard talking and walking with Davis as they pass.

> DAVIS
> Me and Gerald are playing a game of pool tonight.

> MENARD
> Good Davis. I'm glad Bliss's number two and three are willing to get along now.

Vemi smiles.

Bliss is standing with her arms behind her head as she talks to Gerald and watches Vemi's reaction to Menard and Davis.

Vemi still does not see Bliss.

Bliss sees Vemi motion for Man to leave with her.

Bliss and Gerald continue talking as they walk away from the carnival.

(cont'd)

(cont'd)

                    BLISS
G, baby, I apologize. I didn't realize so many things were as they are. My world of want negated my own needs too. It's not just you three that have been hurt by my decisions.

                    GERALD
We know you have feelings, despite the fact you don't show them often. I guess we should be more sensitive to your emotions, just like you should be to ours.

                    BLISS
I'm just as confused as you all are about some of everything going on right now. I'm even thinking about giving the Air Line a two-week notice as soon as I fly out again because I don't want to be flying a plane at five and six months pregnant.

                    GERALD
I think you should have done that a long time ago. It's not like you have to fly planes to eat.

(cont'd)

(cont'd)

EXT. CITY PARK PARKING LOT - DAY

Vemi and Man are laughing and talking.

          VEMI
I wouldn't believe it if I hadn't met you here and ended up seeing and hearing it for myself - and straight from a horse's mouth!

          MAN
So, have I earned my pay and more?

          VEMI
Oh yes. You've earned the pay. Now, more than that, you have a little more to put in complimentary before you can get a yes on that.

          MAN
Is that right? A woman all about whatever business she's focused on at any given time I see.

          VEMI
As it should be.

          MAN
Really?

(cont'd)

(cont'd)

                    VEMI
Really. See, ain't nothing in life free baby, and can't nothing be done alone. Everything costs somebody something, and there's always somebody needing to do something just so we can do whatever it is we want to do.

                    MAN
So, you're a philosopher huh.

                    VEMI
I'm a feel-n-spotter. I know what I know, and what I don't know I can always find out. Independence is the biggest illusion of humanity. That's why I don't mind depending on people when I need to.

                    MAN
What will I have to do for you to depend on me? How much will I have to pay to play around with you?

Man licks his lips.

                    VEMI
Either $500 cash or two damn good favors.

(cont'd)

(cont'd)

                MAN
You already had that answer waiting for me, huh.

                VEMI
I know men if I don't know anything else. You all are so predictable most times.

                MAN
Hey, we can't help ourselves around beautiful women.

                VEMI
Is it because you think we're really beautiful, or is it just because we are women.

                MAN
Maybe both, but more the latter for me. I love women period. A beautiful woman on the outside is a plus, and a beautiful woman on the inside is even better but even more rare.

                VEMI
Which woman am I?

                MAN
A woman. Regardless, I'm a man and I have the cash on me right now and can give it to you.

(cont'd)

(cont'd)

                    VEMI
        I can take it too. But I
        know that later I'll
        need the favors, which I
        will enjoy much more
        than your sex anyway.
        So, I'll be in touch.

Man is shaking his head.

Vemi gets into her car and cranks it.

Man smiles and continues shaking his head.

Vemi drives away and waves.

Man waves good-bye back.

                    MAN
        She's up to nothing but
        no good. But I'm gonna
        see just how bad she can
        be.

Man's keys JINGLE as he tosses them in the air, catches them and walks away.

EXT. CITY PARK CARNIVAL. BUMPER CARS - DAY

Gerald and Bliss have their arms around each other.

They move up in line.

                    GERALD
        The line's moving pretty
        good.

                    BLISS
        Much better than before.

Gerald takes Bliss by the hand and holds her hand between his.

                                (cont'd)

(cont'd)

                    GERALD
Everything life has to offer can be a part of our happiness, Bliss, if you'll allow it.

                    BLISS
I don't restrict life, and you know that. That's mainly our problem now.

                    GERALD
That's not the problem and you know that. The problem is you wanting everything to work for Bliss regardless of all the other people involved.

                    BLISS
Hey, if I don't look out for me, no one else will. I learned that when my parents died after I turned 21.

Bliss looks around as if she's looking for someone.

                    GERALD
What is it?

                    BLISS
Nothing sweetheart. I'll just be glad when Davis and Menard get back so I can sit down.

Bliss and Gerald move up in line.

(cont'd)

(cont'd)

Menard and Davis approach the line, and work their way to Gerald and Bliss in line.

Bliss gets out of line and Davis gets in line.

> **DAVIS**
> Thanks for holding my spot baby.

Davis gives Bliss a quick kiss on the lips.

> **BLISS**
> Not a problem at all. I'm just glad there's still something I can do to make you happy.

> **DAVIS**
> Come on girl. You know you keep me happy. You keep me going, even when you're wrong.

> **BLISS**
> So you say right now! So you say, right now.

Bliss pouts.

> **DAVIS**
> Don't talk like that.

> **GERALD**
> And don't act like that.

> **DAVIS**
> You know you can trust what I say to you, and probably what G and M have to say to you too.

Davis and Gerald move up a few spaces in line.

(cont'd)

(cont'd)

                    BLISS
         I keep forgetting that
         I'm the cause of all our
         problems.

                    DAVIS
         Don't exaggerate baby
         girl. Not all our
         problems, just all the
         recent ones we've been
         having have all been
         because of you.

Davis and Menard laugh.

                    BLISS
         That's not funny.

Gerald and Davis begin to board the bumper cars.

Bliss and Menard walk away from the bumper cars.

They sit on a nearby bench as Gerald and Davis begin their ride.

Both Gerald and Davis notice that Bliss and Menard are talking.

They see Menard put his arm around Bliss.

Gerald and Davis crash their bumper cars into each other.

                    GERALD
         Sorry about that. I
         guess they had your
         attention too.

Gerald backs up his bumper car.

(cont'd)

          DAVIS
Had, still got. I always keep my eyes on Menard when he's with Bliss. Every chance he gets, he inches closer to her. He's cool and all, but that man's been in my way for too long.

Gerald looks at Davis, then looks at Menard with Bliss.

          GERALD
What was going on in Bliss's head to marry all three of us?

          DAVIS
Being happy. That's all she ever wants is to be happy all the time.

          GERALD
Being happy at the expense of nearly all else and everyone else, including herself.

          DAVIS
Yes, but that's our wife.

INT. BLISS'S PLACE. SUNROOM – DAY

Bliss is with Gerald and Davis.

Bliss is sitting in an oversized chaise.

Davis is lying on the sofa.

Gerald is resting in the hammock by the window.

(cont'd)

(cont'd)

BLISS
Yep. We were on the phone all that time just with him trying to tell me all the reasons why everything is better and not worse. Long story short: I'm 12-weeks, and having twins.

GERALD
Huh.

DAVIS
Twelve weeks?

BLISS
And twins.

Davis gets off the sofa, goes to Bliss, and hugs her while he repeatedly kisses her on her neck playfully.

GERALD
I wish I could be that happy about the news.

DAVIS
You can. Just be.

GERALD
I can't. All this does is makes me feel further pushed away from my wife.

DAVIS
We're all family despite how we comprise that family, man.

Davis stands beside Bliss and rubs her stomach.

(cont'd)

(cont'd)

> GERALD
> I feel sick. I can't accept this. Bliss is my wife, and now she's pregnant and I know it's no way those are my kids.

> BLISS
> I instantly knew that too, love. We were together for the first time one month before we got married last month. It hurts, I know.

> GERALD
> That's right. It hurts damn bad.

> BLISS
> And you think I don't know how it feels.

> GERALD
> Got damn right! I don't think you know how bad I feel and I don't think you even care.

Menard enters the room and looks confused.

> MENARD
> What's happening?

> GERALD
> My world keeps crumbling around me, right in my face!

(cont'd)

(cont'd)

                GERALD
               (to Bliss)
        Eight weeks was the
        maximum it could have
        been for you to be
        pregnant by me! All this
        time, I've been thinking
        that you were carrying
        my kids - that it was
        possible for something
        good to come out of my
        marrying you and moving
        in here.

                BLISS
        Something good can come
        out of this.

                GERALD
        Not for me.

                BLISS
        And even that can be a
        good thing, especially
        considering the fact
        that you've pretty much
        had everything work out
        your way all your life.
        This is about the only
        real problem you've had.

                GERALD
        Well, it won't be a
        problem for long.

                DAVIS
        Yo man, calm down.

Menard looks at Bliss as if he is realizing something for the first time.

                MENARD
        So, Bliss found out that
        G's not the father?

                              (cont'd)

(cont'd)

                    BLISS
I'm 12-weeks pregnant with twins.

                    DAVIS
Twins run in my family - fraternal and identical.

                    MENARD
Mine too.

                    DAVIS
Whether or not they're mine, I'm staying by my honey and helping her take care of these babies.

Bliss kisses Davis's cheek and strokes his chin.

                    MENARD
I'm not sure I can say that just yet. I know I hope they're mine and I know I'll take care of them if they are - whether or not I'm with their mom.

Bliss lays her head on Davis's shoulder.

                    GERALD
I'm not sure how much more of this I can take.

Bliss closes her eyes.

                    BLISS
I'm not sure how much more of this I can take either.

(cont'd)

(cont'd)

                GERALD
Why does it seem like you don't give a damn about how I feel?

                BLISS
Because I've been listening to the way you feel for weeks now and nothing has changed. Why can't you think about me for a change, and quit pretending like you always think about me. To you, I matter only because of what I am – somebody helping you fool yourself about your history.

                GERALD
What the hell does that mean?

The doorbell RINGS.

                BLISS
There's the door.

INT. HARDWARE STORE - DAY

The bell BUZZES as a customer enters and walks past Menard.

Menard is standing by the window looking at cans of paint.

Menard picks up a can of metallic silver paint and reads the label.

The STORE CLERK walked up.

(cont'd)

(cont'd)

                  STORE CLERK
        May I help you sir?

                  MENARD
        No ma'am, thank you
        though.

                  STORE CLERK
        Let me know if you
        change your mind.

                  MENARD
        Thank you.

The door bell BUZZES again as another customer enters the store.

Vemi's heels TAP as she walks toward Menard.

Menard looks up as he puts down the can of paint.

He resumes looking at the paint and reaches to pick up another can.

Vemi stops nearly an inch away from Menard.

                  VEMI
        Menard, hello. Remember
        me? Vemi.

                  MENARD
        I'm sorry, I don't.
        Vemi? No.

Menard puts down the can of paint and steps back.

                  MENARD
        How do you know me?
        You're from here in
        Missouri?

(cont'd)

(cont'd)

                VEMI
I'm a flight attendant most times when Bliss flies.

Menard is looking puzzled.

                VEMI
We've never actually met face-to-face before now, but I've seen pictures of you and have seen you around; so I thought you probably remembered my face too.

Menard smiles.

                MENARD
Okay. You seem familiar to me now.

                VEMI
Nice to finally meet you after three years.

                MENARD
Nice meeting you.

Menard and Vemi shake hands.

                VEMI
I would hug you because seem like family to me already. Bliss and I are real tight.

                MENARD
Is that so? Tell me something then.

(cont'd)

(cont'd)

                    VEMI
          What would you like to
          know?

                    MENARD
          What does she say about
          me?

                    VEMI
          She loves you. The other
          two things are so hot
          that I'll have to tell
          you in your ear.

                    MENARD
          Tell me then.

Vemi steps close to Menard and whispers into his ear.

INT. SHOE STORE - DAY

Kimera is by the window looking at shoes. She looks up and sees Vemi whispering in Menard's ear. Kimera stands looking out the window with her hands on her hips.

                    KIMERA
          What is this shit?

INT. HARDWARE STORE - DAY

Vemi finishes whispering in Menard's ear.

She rubs his arm.

She reaches into her purse and pulls out her business card.

                    MENARD
          So, she loves me and
          finds me to me a great
          lover endowed with more
          understanding than any
          other man?

(cont'd)

(cont'd)

                    VEMI
        For the most part. Why
        are you asking?
        Shouldn't you know?

Menard nods his head.

                    MENARD
        I do. A human just has
        questions from time to
        time, especially when
        dealing with Bliss.

INT. SHOE STORE - DAY

Kimera has her arms folded and TAPPING her foot as she continues watching Menard and Vemi talk in the hardware store.

Kimera walks away from the window.

She waves good-bye to the sales associate and leaves the store.

EXT. CITY STREET. HISTORIC DISTRICT - DAY

Kimera is looking angry as she steps from the sidewalk into the street.

A horse and carriage slowly began passing in front of her.

Kimera was forced to stop in the middle of the street.

                    KIMERA
        Is this a movie or
        something?

When the horse and carriage passed, she began walking again and chuckled. As she stepped onto the sidewalk in front of the hardware store, she didn't have a facial expression.

(cont'd)

                    KIMERA
        I don't like Vemi's
        dirty ass. I know she's
        up to no good. I knew
        the moment I saw her.

Kimera enters the hardware store.

INT. HARDWARE STORE - DAY

The door BUZZES when Kimera enters.

Vemi and Menard both look toward the door.

Vemi turns to Menard.

                    VEMI
        Here's Kimera. Call me
        and I'll be straight up
        with you about Bliss.

                    MENARD
        I do need to talk to
        someone. I'll do that.

                    VEMI
        Call tonight. Bye.

Vemi steps away just as Kimera walks up.

                    KIMERA
        Hey! Did I break
        something up?

                    VEMI
        Actually we just met
        when I dipped in real
        quick for some nails.
        Hate to run. See you two
        some other time.

(cont'd)

(cont'd)

                MENARD
Nice meeting you.

Vemi leaves Menard and Kimera.

                MENARD
Kimera, hello. What brings you in here?

                KIMERA
I saw her all over you when I was across the street shopping near the window.

                MENARD
It wasn't like that. She was telling me about some of the things Bliss told her about me. Of course all the stuff she said was good, so she probably made that up.

                KIMERA
Man, stay away from Vemi. She's not a friend of Bliss, and she's not a friend of yours or anybody else.

                MENARD
You two acted like you were friends.

                KIMERA
No, we acted acquainted with each other, which we are. We're not friends. I've had a bad feeling about her since I first met her at the movies a while back. She's up to something.

                              (cont'd)

(cont'd)

                    MENARD
        You're just like Bliss.
        Any woman other than you
        or her has a hidden
        agenda.

                    KIMERA
        Just like not all men
        are bad, not all women
        are bad. And nobody is
        good all the time. Bliss
        and I are good women who
        are bad sometimes. Vemi
        is one of those bad
        women who are good
        sometimes.

                    MENARD
        I hear you. You're not
        friends.

                    KIMERA
        More important, she's
        not your friend and she
        sure isn't Bliss's
        friend.

INT. KIMERA'S CAR - DAY

Bone Crusher's "Never Scared" is playing on her radio.

Kimera is driving and talking on her cell phone.

                    KIMERA
        I could have broken her
        neck!

Kimera looks angry.

(cont'd)

(cont'd)

                    KIMERA
          But check this out. I
          went shopping and found
          some hella shoes right,
          but passed them up to go
          across the stree to the
          hardware store to fight
          Vemi off Menard.

Bliss bucks her eyes. Kimera nods her head.

                    KIMERA
          Yeap. She apparently
          approached him at the
          store. She left when I
          walked up, and they were
          saying nice meeting you
          to each other.

Bliss leans her head left. Kimera nods her head again.

                    KIMERA
          You might think so, but
          I believe she already
          knew he was your husband
          and she went to him to
          give him her number
          because she whipped it
          out quick.

Bliss shifts in her seat. Kimera nods her head again.

                    KIMERA
          Handle that. I told him
          to not talk to her again
          because you two weren't
          friends, but you handle
          this from here. Just let
          me know if you need me
          to beat Vemi down for
          you.

(cont'd)

(cont'd)

INT. AIRPLANE - DAY

Vemi is talking to James.

          JAMES
You have to be kidding me.

Their flight ends and they are standing by the doorway and bidding the passengers farewell.

Vemi and James walk through the empty airplane talking and picking up items left on the floor and in the seats.

          VEMI
The first one is coming over to my place tomorrow night.

          JAMES
I can't believe you're doing that.

          VEMI
I'm just gonna let him talk to me. He thinks we're friends, and Miss Thang's got his brain scattered. I'm just gonna help him figure some things out.

          JAMES
You're sounding like you have a date to break up a marriage.

          VEMI
I'm just trying to find out some things, and have fun.

James shakes his head in disbelief.

          (cont'd)

(cont'd)

                    JAMES
Based on what you said and the way you said it, it sounds like you were flirting with him and made him curious so he would call you.

                    VEMI
So you just have it all figured out, don't you?

                    JAMES
And I know he's not gonna leave her. Her stuff's together.

                    VEMI
My leg's out. She'll fall.

FADE OUT

INT. BLISS'S HOME. BALLROOM - DAY

Menard is breaking up a fight between Gerald and Davis.

                    MENARD
                    (yelling)
Stop! I'm not having this shit in this house!

Gerald runs and grabs a sword from the shield on the wall.

Davis runs and grabs the other sword next to the shield.

                    GERALD
                    (yelling)
Come on bad ass! Come on!

(cont'd)

(cont'd)

Gerald and Davis begin fencing. Menard grabs one of the rifles from the rack and pumps it.

Gerald and Davis stop fighting, and stand ready to fight with swords still in hand.

                  GERALD
     I'm tired of being
     fucked with!

                  DAVIS
       (yelling)
     Leave bitch!

Gerald laughs.

                  GERALD
     You wish bitch! As if
     that'll make your life
     any easier. I intimidate
     you. That's all it is. I
     intimidate you.

Gerald turns his back to walk away.

                  DAVIS
     No you don't. I just
     don't like white people.

Gerald faces Davis and shakes his head in disagreement.

                  MENARD
     Bliss is unfunny like
     that - exposing wounds
     and dousing them with
     gasoline. This is not
     worth it men. Stop the
     race hating. And stop
     the fighting over a
     woman so selfish she
     would never even think
     about fighting over you.

                                  (cont'd)

(cont'd)

INT. COURTHOUSE - DAY

Bliss is standing at the counter beneath a sign that says "Divorces."

The COUNTER AGENT returns and hands Bliss some papers.

                    BLISS
          Does that take care of
          everything?

                  COUNTER AGENT
          Yes, everything as far
          as the legal paper
          trail.

                    BLISS
          So, now what?

                  COUNTER AGENT
         Well, all I can tell you
          to do is to notify your
          domestic partners that
          the dissolution has
          taken place, and inform
          your husband of your
          divorce. Other than
          that, I can only hope
          you enjoy being single
          more than I do.

The counter agent turns up her nose at Bliss.

                  COUNTER AGENT
          And all I want is one
          husband. I only need one
          fire burning.

Bliss looks bothered.

                                          (cont'd)

(cont'd)

                    BLISS
            Good to know.

Bliss TAPS the stack of papers on the counter top.

                    BLISS
            Well, thank you ma'am
            for all of your help
            with taking care of this
            paperwork for me so
            quickly, and especially
            for your well-wishing. I
            pray you will be able to
            love someone who loves
            and accepts you forever.

Bliss turns and strolls away smiling and looking at her papers.

She passes the police officer securing the exit as he talks to another man who was leaving the building.

                    BLISS
            Enjoy your evening you
            two.

The officer and man both smile at Bliss.

The officer waves his hand.

The man tips his hat.

EXT. COURTHOUSE - DAY

Bliss is looking at the papers as she walks to her blue Bentley.

Her keys JINGLE as she pulls them out of her pocket and searches for the car key.

She looks at the papers as she unlocks the car door and as she gets in and puts the keys in the ignition.

                                      (cont'd)

(cont'd)

                    BLISS
          I'm so me right now!
          Happiness is! Now
          nothing they do or say
          will have any reason to
          matter.

Bliss CRANKS the car. She CLICKS her seatbelt then begins driving away.

EXT. BLISS'S HOME - DAY

The sun and moon can both be seen.

Menard is leaning and talking to two men in a white Hummer. Davis is behind the wheel and Gerald is in the passenger seat. Menard stands up straight and laughs as he hits the Hummer.

                    MENARD
          Just be sure to drive
          safe. I want to know you
          made it without getting
          hurt, and I want you to
          make sure you make it
          back here before Bliss
          notices anything
          tomorrow morning.

All three men are laughing as Gerald CLICKS his seatbelt, then Davis CLICKS his belt.

                    MENARD
          I'm beginning to hate
          that this whole month
          and half here has been
          total hell for you G.
          But I won't pretend that
          I'm not happy to see one
          of my problems with my
          wife leave. I'm just
          sorry she caused you the
          same problem though,
          pretty much.

                              (cont'd)

(cont'd)

Menard extends his right hand past Davis.

Gerald and Menard shake hands.

> **GERALD**
> She's causing us all the same problems until we do something about it. Hopefully I'm not a day too late because I want to get this thing annulled then get on with my life.

Menard puts his hands into his pockets and bends over as he looks up.

Davis turns to Gerald and begins talking.

> **DAVIS**
> You're a pretty cool cat when it's all said and done. I can see why Bliss went for you out of all the other white men that try to get with her. I'm sorry I gave you that much grief man. This woman's got me dealing with a lot of things.

> **GERALD**
> Hey, if I hadn't married her and moved here, I wouldn't believe it if you would have told every detail to me. I was taking frustrations out on you guys too. I guess she made us all crazy, or just found us that way one.

(cont'd)

(cont'd)

The three men laugh again as Davis CRANKS the Hummer and pulls off as Gerald waves.

Menard stands in the yard waving as the Hummer leaves the driveway.

The hummer disappears down the long road.

The phone RINGS and Menard walks into the house.

INT. BLISS'S HOME. FOYER - DAY.

Menard is standing in front of a mirror. He notices his reflection and looks directly at it as he answers the phone.

                MENARD
          This is Menard.

He gives a smile that seems inquisitive or doubtful. He grabs a nearby notepad and pen.

                MENARD
         How do I get there?

Menard rests the phone on his shoulder as he writes directions.

                MENARD
         I am only free for the
         next couple of hours. Is
         now good for you?

Menard finishes writing and tears the note from the pad before putting the pad and pen back where he noticed them first.

                MENARD
         I'm on my way in 10
         minutes.

(cont'd)

(cont'd)

Menard hangs up the phone and walks away.

The phone RINGS again.

          MENARD
          (yelling)
    What kid sis!

He walks back to the phone. The phone RINGS a half before Menard answers it.

          MENARD
    This is Menard.

He rests the phone on his shoulder and looks at the note he'd written a moment prior.

          MENARD
    So I don't need to come
    because he's there now,
    right?

Menard puts the note in the trash can.

          MENARD
    Somehow I figured you'd
    gotten impatient on him.
    You need more faith and
    less panic, but I still
    love you kid sis. Call
    me when you need me.

Menard hangs up the phone and looks up at his reflection in the mirror.

          MENARD
    Bliss and I can still
    have the perfectly
    loving home we grew up
    in.

                          (cont'd)

(cont'd)

Menard stares at his reflection.

> MENARD
> Bliss and I will raise
> our twin girls here,
> with it being just us.

Menard stares at his reflection then finally blinks.

> MENARD
> I love her. I'm not
> leaving her.

INT. VEMI'S PLACE. BEDROOM - NIGHT

Vemi is taking off a red dress as her reflection shows in the full-length mirror.

> VEMI
> Light the fireplace if
> you want.

INT. VEMI'S PLACE. LIVING ROOM - NIGHT

Menard is sitting on the couch looking at Vemi's card.

INT. VEMI'S PLACE. BEDROOM - NIGHT

Vemi zips a pair of jeans and pulls on a shirt.

INT. VEMI'S PLACE. LIVING ROOM - NIGHT

Menard puts Vemi's card in his shirt pocket.

The door POPS and CREEKS as Vemi opens it to walk out of the bedroom into the living room.

Menard stands up and adjusts the pillows on Vemi's couch as Vemi strolls and stops an inch from him.

(cont'd)

(cont'd)

                    VEMI
          I'm glad you called and
          came by.

Vemi steps away from Menard.

                    VEMI
          Can I get you something
          to drink? Want something
          to snack on or something
          real to eat?

Menard sits back on the couch.

                    MENARD
          Not trying to be funny,
          but I don't eat and
          drink with people the
          first few times I spend
          time with them. I have
          to get to know with whom
          I'm breaking bread.

Vemi sits on the couch.

                    VEMI
          That sounds so Bliss.

                    MENARD
          It is part Bliss.

                    VEMI
          Umph.

Vemi scoots closer to Menard and crosses her legs.

                    VEMI
          Now, what's bothering
          you? What are you trying
          to understand about my
          girl Bliss that you
          aren't already aware of?

                                    (cont'd)

(cont'd)

Vemi rubs Menard's face.

She then slides her legs apart and re-crosses them.

          MENARD
I love Bliss, to death. I just don't understand how she can love me the same way, yet marry two other men and move them in with us.

Vemi tries to not look happy to hear Menard make that confession.

Vemi strokes Menard's hair.

INT. KIMERA'S PLACE - NIGHT

Bliss is drinking an apple juice and sitting on the love seat.

Kimera is pouring a glass of red wine.

She puts the bottle on the floor next to the couch.

She sits on the other end of the couch and sips the wine.

          BLISS
Lord, in the name of Jesus, I pray that you please continue guiding me despite my being less than what you made.

          KIMERA
Amen!

          BLISS
Jah, I thank you for all that you've done for me.

(cont'd)

(cont'd)

                    KIMERA
          Amen.

Both ladies drink her respective beverage.

Kimera walks over to a window and peeks through the wood blinds.

                    KIMERA
          We need to pray that ole
          girl of Funchess doesn't
          roll through here again.

Kimera stops looking outside.

                    BLISS
          Is that what happened to
          your mailbox?

                    KIMERA
          Yep. She ran over it,
          then got out of her car
          and stood there with a
          gun waiting pointed at
          my front door.

Kimera goes to sit back on the couch.

                    KIMERA
          Jah, in the name of
          Jesus I thank you for
          saving my life by
          sending your Holy Spirit
          to tell me to look
          outside from my bathroom
          window and don't walk
          past the living room
          window or open the front
          door!

(cont'd)

(cont'd)

                    BLISS
          Yes, thank you Jesus!
          Praise Jah!

Kimera steps over the bottle of wine on the floor and sits back in her spot on the couch.

                    KIMERA
          But Bliss, girl, I was so mad when I noticed that Funchess had his punk tail sitting in there on the passenger side. I wanted to go out there so bad, but I knew I didn't have no gun!

                    BLISS
          Don't tell me that you went and bought a gun.

                    KIMERA
          Nah, I still don't have one, but I know that if I see that bitch face-to-face, I'm taking her down if I have to take hers from her.

Bliss puts down her juice.

                    BLISS
          Now Kimera, no man is worth fighting over. Having no man is better than having a raggedy piece of man any day, and you know that.

(cont'd)

(cont'd)

                KIMERA
Oh, I broke up with him a couple of days ago. I don't want him. He's mad because he still wants me.

                BLISS
What?

                KIMERA
Girl, yeah, mad for real. He told me that he'll tell her about me, and keep her thinking we're together until we do get back together. He knew she would start going crazy and stalking me for him.

                BLISS
It's good you left him alone girl. He sounds dangerously in a selfish love for you.

                KIMERA
That's the perfect way to summarize what I put together the other day! He doesn't love me: he loves the way he feels when he's with me. I am not a person he loves, I am an experience he loves to be connected to. His love is his wife. I can no longer give him my life.

(cont'd)

(cont'd)

BLISS
Praise God for revelation!

INT. VEMI'S PLACE - NIGHT

Menard is looking at the pictures on Vemi's wall.

Vemi is on the couch looking at Menard.

VEMI
Bliss is the kind of woman who can't appreciate a man like you the right way.

MENARD
How can you be her friend and say something like that?

VEMI
Friends know each other, and it's because I not only know Bliss, but know how chaotic she can be, that I can tell you that she'll never change. That's the only thing constant about her.

Menard stops looking at the pictures and faces Vemi with his arms behind his back.

MENARD
You talk a good game. Too good, as a matter of fact. What are you trying to do? Why did you approach me at the hardware store?

(cont'd)

(cont'd)

> VEMI
> I want to make love to you.

> MENARD
> To make love, we must have love. You and I don't love each other.

> VEMI
> Have you not loved me since meeting me at the hardware store?

> MENARD
> I have not. My only thoughts regarding you were all connected to my wife and what you can tell me about her.

Vemi gets off the couch and walks over to Menard.

> MENARD
> Please back away from me.

Menard smiles.

> MENARD
> I like you, and right now I'm feeling a lot of different emotions and don't want to do the wrong thing.

> VEMI
> Like what? Bend me over and fuck me?

(cont'd)

(cont'd)

                MENARD
If I wasn't married, you would be right.

Menard steps away from Vemi.

                VEMI
How can you be faithful to someone who is obviously not being faithful to you and doesn't appreciate you?

                MENARD
It's not hard because I know she does appreciate me, and love me, regardless. Everytime my heart beats, I remember the vows we made to each other, and I believe that she'll soon come to her senses and she'll realize her love is with me and only me. She's just been through a lot in her life.

                VEMI
You are the world's trillionth hopeful romantic. And if the babies she's carrying turn out to not be yours, what are you going to do?

(cont'd)

(cont'd)

> MENARD
> I don't know. I know that when I think about it right now, I feel like I will stay with her regardless of whether they're my twins or not. I don't want to ever be the one to cause Bliss pain.

> VEMI
> If only she felt that way about you.

Menard looks angry.

> MENARD
> Before, you acted like she did - saying she loves me and all that stuff. I guess you were just playing your little role, huh. You don't want Bliss and I to work anything out.

> VEMI
> What I want is for you to be happy. You deserve at least that much from life.

> MENARD
> I'm happy. True, not everything is the way I want it to be, but then nothing has ever been that way for me.

Menard picks up his keys.

(cont'd)

(cont'd)

VEMI
Just know that if you need to talk to someone, always come to me. I want to be here to give you whatever you need.

MENARD
You were a great help tonight, and I'm glad I met you Vemi, but I won't be calling you again. I feel you're more harm than help to me and Bliss.

Menard steps past Vemi.

He places Vemi's card on the coffee table.

She looks surprised and disappointed.

VEMI
Menard, don't do this. Stay for a little while longer. All your troubles can end tonight.

MENARD
(laughing)
No. If I stay, all my troubles will increase tonight.

Menard walks toward the door.

Vemi tries to stop Menard and falls to the floor with her arms around his legs.

VEMI
Don't leave me!

(cont'd)

(cont'd)

                    MENARD
          Let go. If only you were
          Bliss, and I loved you
          like I love her.

Vemi's still on the floor hanging on to Menard's leg and looking up at him with tears in her eyes.

                    VEMI
          You and I have more in
          common than you and
          Bliss does. Be with me!
          I can show you how a man
          like you should be
          treated.

                    MENARD
          I've already been shown
          that, and that's how I
          know that I need to get
          my household back if I
          want that from my wife
          again. I have to go. Let
          go.

Vemi lets go of Menard's leg and begins crying on the floor.

                    MENARD
          Come on, get up. Don't
          do that.

                    VEMI
                (crying)
          Just leave! You don't
          give a damn about me,
          even though I have shown
          you that I care so much
          for you already!

(cont'd)

(cont'd)

                    MENARD
I'm sorry, but I love my wife and I don't want another woman, especially not a friend of hers.

Menard extends his hand to help Vemi to her feet.

                    VEMI
         (sniffing)
Just go Menard. I tried to help you. Just go!

                    MENARD
I don't want to leave you like this.

                    VEMI
         (crying)
Why? You don't give a damn about me.

                    MENARD
Because you're a friend of Bliss, I do care about you. I want to be sure you're alright before I leave. I didn't mean to lead you on then hurt your feelings. I shouldn't have come over.

Vemi stands to her feet and wipes the tears from her face.

                    VEMI
Why not just leave Bliss and come to be with me?

(cont'd)

(cont'd)

> MENARD
> I neither know nor like you that way. We can't talk again. I really feel like even coming here tonight was a huge mistake. I feel like you're up to something, and I'm just a pawn you're trying to position.

> VEMI
> Bliss has been positioning you all this time, so why not let me?

> MENARD
> I am no one's game piece.

Menard opens the door and walks out.

Vemi runs to the doorway and yells down the hall at Menard.

> VEMI
> (yelling)
> I see why she's making a fool out of you! You'll regret doing this to me big time!

Vemi SLAMS the door.

INT. BLISS'S HOME. SITTING ROOM - NIGHT

The door opens and Menard steps in the room.

Bliss is naked and lounging on the chaise as she reads from the white book of poetry and has the yellow book opened and turned face down in her lap.

(cont'd)

(cont'd)

Menard stands and stares at Bliss for a short while.

Bliss never looks away from the book.

> BLISS
> Enjoy yourself?

> MENARD
> It was okay, more informative than fun.

> BLISS
> Is that so?

Menard JINGLES the keys as he keeps looking at Bliss and sits in the oversized chair near her chaise.

> MENARD
> Was your day good?

> BLISS
> It was. More informative than fun, but it was a great day overall.

> MENARD
> Did you hang out with Kimera tonight?

> BLISS
> Yes. Did you go to see Vemi tonight? Yes.

> MENARD
> Yes. She called you and told you?

Bliss closes the book and looks at Menard.

(cont'd)

(cont'd)

                    BLISS
Vemi doesn't have any of my numbers. We just see each other when she's working on a plane I'm flying. Why were you talking to her at the hardware store and over to her house tonight?

                    MENARD
I thought she was your friend, and I just went to get advice from her on our situations here.

                    BLISS
You better be lying to me!

Bliss puts the white book of poetry next to the lamp.

                    MENARD
She walked up to me at the store and told me she was your friend, and that you loved me and she could help me.

                    BLISS
Help you what!

Bliss removes the yellow poetry book from her lap and places it on the table between she and Menard.

                    MENARD
Understand you more, know that you love me for real, hell I don't know. I don't know nothing anymore.

(cont'd)

(cont'd)

                    BLISS
          Oh, so did she screw your brains out? What the hell were you doing at her house!

Bliss sits straight up on the end of the chaise.

                    MENARD
          Your antics made me lose my mind. I told you I went over there thinking she was your friend and we were going to talk about why you do the things you do. Instead, I get there and she starts trying to give it to me, and gets to talking about how you're not what I need.

Bliss crosses her arms.

                    BLISS
          Um huh. What you think?

                    MENARD
          So I left. I put her business card on her coffee table, and I walked out on her. I told her I love you and don't even want to look at another woman.

                    BLISS
          I'm so glad I did what I did today. And since tomorrow is my last flight for the next year, I'll just have to give Miss Vemi Esmarelda a bit of recompense.

                                    (cont'd)

(cont'd)

Bliss gets up and walks out of the room.

Menard has a look on his face that says he's both afraid and relieved.

Menard looks around the room.

He picks up the white book of poetry, then the yellow book of poetry.

He begins reading from the white book.

                MENARD
        Page 40. Shadowing the
        love hidden behind
        eyes/Showing them all
        the heart inside/Shaking
        the world for the titles
        it tries/Showering
        stitch and confusion
        while strolling through
        lives.

Menard lifts his eyebrows and flips through the pages.

                MENARD
        Page 76. The Sweet
        Heart. How sweet do you
        like your
        tea/hearty/even this can
        not fully contain love
        from me in its or my
        entirety/so what shall
        it be/one/four/or
        eight/lumps of pumps of
        me.

Menard closes the book.

(cont'd)

(cont'd)

                    MENARD
          Damn. Two for two. This
          is some relative and
          damn good poetry! No
          wonder Bliss seems to be
          getting better and is
          more devoted to reading
          these books than to
          engaging us men in our
          drama.

He looks at the cover, then flips the book over. He then begins reading the back cover before putting it down.

Menard then picks up the yellow book. He looks at the back cover, then opens it to Page 2.

                    MENARD
          Whoa. The title is Her.
          None is she like/Though
          character and features
          may resemble/Her nature
          is delight/Yet with all
          she's cautious and
          nimble/Sage is she/
          Making years of life
          give others shock/
          Eloquence flows
          naturally /Intuition
          serves as her master to
          all locks/Words spoken/
          Bring a truth others
          have happily sought/A
          true token/ Loving souls
          over things that can be
          bought/Stretching high/
          As postured as a
          century-old pine/Ending
          the lie/That beauty
          never-ever couples a
          smart mind/Seemingly

(cont'd)

(cont'd)

> MENARD (cont'd)
> always flying above/The ailments of life-whole and part/Capable of giving the deepest love/but will not ever risk damaging her heart.

Menard closes the book.

> MENARD
> I finally understand Bliss. Just like she lost her mother before moving in with her father, then he died, she knows one day I'll die.

Menard puts the books together on Bliss's chaise.

> MENARD
> That's why she married me and Davis almost at the same time. She's just afraid to love me and lose me. I have to let her know that I'm not going anywhere, and Davis and Gerald have to go, forever.

Menard gets up and walks out of the room.

EXT. AIRPORT - DAY

Bliss parks her Bentley.

As she is walking from the parking lot, she and sees Vemi.

Bliss looks at Vemi run across the street.

(cont'd)

(cont'd)

Vemi is ahead of Bliss and does not see Bliss.

Vemi stops before walking inside the airport.

She primps as she looks at her reflection in the glass.

>			VEMI
> These foolish ass men
> don't know a thing.

Vemi shakes her hair and adjusts her uniform.

She walks inside.

Bliss walks across the street.

The wind blows her hair.

Bliss leans her head and moves her hair off her face.

The airport doors slide open.

Bliss puts her hat on her head.

She walks inside the airport.

>			BLISS
> Showtime.

INT. AIRPLANE - DAY

A MALE PILOT runs up to Bliss.

Bliss stops walking and begins smiling.

(cont'd)

(cont'd)

>MALE PILOT
>The boss is looking for you, James and Vemi. He's trying to let Vemi know to excuse herself from the flight because her house is on fire. You and James will have to go at it alone these two flights tonight.

>BLISS
>Not a problem.

>MALE PILOT
>I tried to catch Vemi to let her know to go home, but she didn't hear me calling out to her.

>BLISS
>(laughing)
>She was just a bit ahead of me. You should have run a bit faster huh?

>MALE PILOT
>Tell me about it. I know she lives alone, and everything's probably already lost by now, but the sooner she gets home, the better for her.

>BLISS
>I agree.

>MALE PILOT
>Tell her the boss said to go home for the night?

(cont'd)

(cont'd)

                    BLISS
          I will.

Bliss walks away.

                MALE PILOT
          Thanks a lot. Sorry
          about Vemi's house, and
          sorry for you and James
          for being stuck handling
          full flights short
          handed.

                    BLISS
          Thank you. Enjoy your
          flights.

                MALE PILOT
          You too. And,
          congratulations on the
          early maternity leave.
          I'll be seeing you next
          year.

                    BLISS
          Indeed. Thank you.

The male pilot walks away.

Bliss walks down the hallway to board the plane.

INT. AIRPLANE - DAY

Bliss boards the plane.

James greets her and opens the cockpit door for her.

                    JAMES
          Bliss! Hello! As always,
          it is a pleasure to see
          you again.

(cont'd)

(cont'd)

          BLISS
You as well.

Bliss steps inside the cockpit.

James rests on the door.

          JAMES
The talk is the good news. Why'd you keep it from us? I heard you're about five months pregnant and tonight's your last two flights for a year.

          BLISS
You know I'm rather private.

          JAMES
That's true.

          BLISS
So it's not that I kept it from you guys. It just never really came up. I guess we can say the opportunity to discuss what really happens in our private lives don't really present themselves. We have just enough time to say hello and possibly toss out summaries of time at home.

(cont'd)

(cont'd)

                JAMES
             (laughing)
       That's definitely the way it is, just like now. Get us to our destination pilot.

Bliss salutes James.

                BLISS
       Yes sir! Have our passengers to get bucked and ready for take-off in five.

James stands at attention and salutes Bliss.

James then nods his head and proceeds to close the door.

Vemi walks up and keeps the door from closing.

James steps back.

Vemi and Bliss wave at each other.

                BLISS
            (sarcastic)
       You can go home. Your house is on fire. James and I will handle tonight's flights with ease. Go take care of home.

                VEMI
            (smurking)
       If it's already on fire, there's nothing I can do about it right? Thank you for trying to give me the night off though. I think I'll just stay here and enjoy my friend's last night.

                                 (cont'd)

(cont'd)

> **BLISS**
> We're not friends Vemi. You need to quit saying that we are. We're cordial business associates at best.

James walks away.

Bliss sits in the pilot's seat.

Vemi is still standing in the doorway looking at Bliss.

> **VEMI**
> I'm going to ignore that remark. It's just your hormones are off kilter and it's beginning to get to you.

> **BLISS**
> I'm fine health wise. Emotionally, I'm a threat to your life, so you might want to close my cockpit door before I have to come close it.

> **VEMI**
> What did I do to you that has you suddenly acting like this toward me?

> **BLISS**
> Vemi, I know about how you're trying to create more chaos in my home. You can't trick a magician spectator. Menard is mine and I am his, forever.

(cont'd)

(cont'd)

VEMI
Honey, I don't even want your husband. I wouldn't have him.

BLISS
No, he wouldn't have you! You wanted him bad enough to throw yourself at him hard enough for him to give you back your phone number!

VEMI
Believe what you want.

Bliss looks angry and gets up from her chair.

Vemi looks nonchalant.

Bliss moves fast toward Vemi.

Vemi SHUTS the cockpit door.

EXT. BLISS'S HOME - DAY

The black Hummer pulls into the driveway.

Menard is outside caring for the lawn.

Davis and Gerald wave from the Hummer.

Davis stops driving and Gerald gets out in front.

MENARD
So how did it all go?

GERALD
I'll have to tell you once we're all inside. You won't believe what ended up happening.

(cont'd)

(cont'd)

Davis parks the Hummer in a rear garage.

Menard and Gerald walk inside the house.

Davis jogs back to the front of the house, then goes in, looks back and SHUTS the door.

INT. BLISS'S HOME. GAMEROOM - DAY

Davis and Menard are playing table hockey.

Gerald is playing a video game.

GERALD
As hard as it is to believe, it's true. She did it.

DAVIS
We viewed the actual documents man. G's idea to annul his marriage to Bliss lead us in a whole new direction when he changed his mind half-way to the damn airport.

GERALD
The same clerk who helped her process the divorces is the one who told us about the divorces and showed us the paperwork. She wasn't impressed with Bliss. She also told us something else. Something major. She said this property sits on land in four states. This place is famous for a wing in each state.

(cont'd)

(cont'd)

> **MENARD**
> I know you said that the official documents say she was never married to the two of you and that she ended the domestic partnerships with you two, but are you sure that the papers said she divorced me the same day she went to the courthouse and ended it with you?

Menard quits playing the game.

> **GERALD**
> That's right. You don't mean any more to her than we do. She ditched us all, and didn't tell us; yet she made it a point to tell us each a different address for home.

> **DAVIS**
> Maybe she was going to tell us when she got back.

> **MENARD**
> Or maybe she wasn't going to tell us period.

> **GERALD**
> Well, I'll be gone when she gets back. I just wanted to get my last few things and tell you man-to-man how Bliss made things go down. I hate we had to meet like this guys.

(cont'd)

(cont'd)

DAVIS
I hate she dismissed me right along with you two. I really love her.

MENARD
Not more than I love her.

Gerald shakes his head.

GERALD
Lately, I've been wondering why I loved her, or even if I ever really did love her. Asking questions like that, I guess it's good that all this happened and things didn't work out for me to be with Bliss. Some things just aren't meant to be, at least that's the way I'll explain it to my family.

DAVIS
And nothing happens that's not meant to happen, whether or not we like it. I'm glad to have met you G, but I'm also glad to see you leave.

Davis and Gerald laugh and shake hands as Menard looks on angrily.

INT. AIRPLANE - DAY

Vemi and James are shaking hands behind the curtain.

(cont'd)

                JAMES
It's a deal then. You'll finally give up on scheming against Bliss.

Bliss is heard pleasantly preparing the passengers for landing.

                BLISS
It has been an honor to be your pilot. I hope you enjoyed your flight.

James and Vemi look at each other.

Vemi pretends to gag.

She then points her fingers like a gun toward the intercom.

                VEMI
Fire! Boom! Boom! Since we're not friends.

                JAMES
Your know, speaking of fire, how do you know Bliss wasn't serious about you taking the night off because your house is on fire. I couldn't take a chance at not believing her. I really believe she must have been telling you the truth because why would she say something like your house is on fire if it's not on fire?

(cont'd)

(cont'd)

> VEMI
> (adjusting her uniform)
> But how would she know if my house if on fire? Plus, since she said it with all that attitude, I took it to be that she was trying to hex me or something or be funny or something to get me to leave so she can say I abandoned the flight and I lose my job.

> JAMES
> I understand your logic. When you're backstabbing, you do need eyes in the back of your head. But if I were you, I would have gotten off the plane and went straight to the office to call some family or something to find out about my house.

> VEMI
> I'll call when we land just so I can ease your mind and prove to you that Bliss was just saying that to be ugly.

James stands up and adjusts his pants.

> JAMES
> Be sure to do that. I sure hope you're right though. But if you are burned out, my wife and I will do what we can to help you get on your feet.

(cont'd)

(cont'd)

> **VEMI**
> Now you're a friend. Thank you.

> **JAMES**
> I am a friend to you because you're a friend to me. Maybe if you would be that way with her, you could have a relationship like ours.

James puts his hands on the curtain. Vemi puts her hands on the curtain then removes them.

> **VEMI**
> I don't care about Bliss, and never have.

> **JAMES**
> Therein lies all the problems between the two of you. You never gave her a chance and now she's not willing to give you another one.

> **VEMI**
> It's not like I'll miss spending time with her.

> **JAMES**
> That's a sad thing. You two are so much alike. Both of you need to learn that although life will bring bad your way, you also will get back all the bad stuff you do to other people. The law of reciprocity is for real. Nothing you do to someone will go unpunished.

(cont'd)

(cont'd)

James opens the curtain and walks out.

Vemi stands behind the curtain and watches James prepare the passengers for the landing.

Vemi looks afraid.

> VEMI
> My house. The curling iron! I started putting on my make-up, and then my clothes, and never went back to turn it, or the steam iron off. Where was my mind? My house can't be gone behind Bliss's own burning house. I can't be homeless.

The plane stops.

INT. AIRPLANE. COCKPIT – NIGHT

Bliss is talking into a hand-held recorder. She sounds like she is performing poetry.

> BLISS
> What I feel . . . is . . . a . . . . . . pain. A . . . hurt so sharp, I can feel each cut through my belly. I need medical attention.

Bliss rises from her seat and gathers her items.

She opens the cockpit door and staggers as she exits the cockpit.

(cont'd)

(cont'd)

INT. AIRPORT - NIGHT.

Ty is near the ticket counter talking to a co-worker.

He looks up as he comments and his co-worker turns and looks over his shoulders.

Bliss is approaching with her bags.

Ty pats his friend on the shoulder and walks away, toward Bliss.

                TY
        Beautiful Bliss, hello,
        let me help you.

Ty takes her bags from her hands.

                BLISS
        Thank you. You're off?

                TY
        Fasho. You?

                BLISS
        Have one more tonight,
        but in about an hour and
        a half.

                TY
        That's a lot of down
        time. What are your
        plans?

                BLISS
        Let's get me to the
        doctor.

Bliss and Ty begin walking and talking.

Vemi sees them leave the airport together.

(cont'd)

(cont'd)

Vemi walks over to a payphone. She dials and waits for someone to answer.

          VEMI
Hey! Where's your mom?

          9-YEAR-OLD CHILD
              (O.S)
Gone to your house. She said it is on fire.

          VEMI
I'm not at home. I didn't know my house was on fire. When your mother calls back, tell her I'm in another city working. Tell your mom I won't be home for another two and a half hours.

          9-YEAR-OLD CHILD
              (O.S)
Okay Miss Vemi. I'm sorry. We love you.

          VEMI
Thank you baby. I love you too. I think you and your family are the only ones who do love me sometimes. I love you.

Vemi hangs up the phone and begins to cry.

James sees her and walks up to her and hugs her. He holds her tight.

          JAMES
Vemi, I am so sorry that this happened to you.

                              (cont'd)

(cont'd)

                    VEMI
                (crying)
        I didn't know she was
        telling me the truth. I
        could have been home.
        Now, I'm stuck here for
        another 90 minutes while
        who knows what happens
        to my place!

People begin walking by and looking at Vemi.

                    VEMI
                (crying)
        What are you looking at!

                    JAMES
        (still holding Vemi)
        Shhh. Don't. Be good.
        Now is a bad time for
        you. Acting like that
        can only make it worse.
        Be good Vemi. Don't work
        yourself up. Things will
        work out. I love you.
        Your family loves you.
        Your other friends love
        you. There are people
        taking care of your
        place. You'll recover
        just fine from whatever
        damage has been done.

Vemi breaks from James's hug.

                    VEMI
                (wiping her eyes)
        Love don't pay no bills
        though. I might not have
        a thing when I get home
        - no shelter, no food,
        no clothes, no hope.

(cont'd)

(cont'd)

James walks toward Vemi.

                    JAMES
There is always hope when you have faith. We all do things we shouldn't do, but as long as you are willing to change and you believe in and praise God, things will always work out. My wife has divorced me. I'll be fine eventually.

                    VEMI
    (hugging James)
I'm sorry. I didn't know.

                    JAMES
  (hugging Vemi back)
I didn't let you know. It happened around the same time you and all this Bliss business started six months ago. I've been struggling in an expensive apartment since then. You can be my roommate if you need want to do that while you get back on your feet.

                    VEMI
    (laughing)
It'll be a lot cheaper than being on my own, so why not.

                                          (cont'd)

(cont'd)

INT. HOSPITAL - NIGHT.

Bliss and Ty are walking toward each other.

Ty hugs her and asks her something.

Bliss nods her head.

Ty and Bliss hug as they leave the hospital and Bliss begins crying.

INT. AIRPORT - NIGHT

Ty and Bliss hug as they enter the airport together smiling and talking.

Ty and Bliss stop hugging and go their separate ways.

INT. AIRPLANE - NIGHT

James and Vemi are greeting boarding passengers.

Bliss gets in line with the passengers to board the plane.

Bliss boards and is greeted by James and not by Vemi.

> BLISS
> (to Vemi)
> I'll try to get us home in 30 minutes, but 45 minutes will be the latest. I apologize for any loss you've incurred. I too have lost something precious today. If there's anything I can to do help you, let me know.

Bliss walks away, enters the cockpit and the DOOR SHUTS.

(cont'd)

(cont'd)

INT. BLISS'S HOME - NIGHT

Gerald is hugging Bliss.

Menard and Davis are shaking hands.

Gerald shakes hands with Davis and then with Menard.

          BLISS
Gerald, I'm glad that you said that you loved me and didn't want to be without me, but now that I've told you that I didn't want to be with you and you're leaving, I feel like we both can have the chance to be happy with the life and love we have left to give.

Davis gives Gerald a set of keys.

          BLISS
Take the white Expedition with you. I don't need a big vehicle like that anymore. The title is already signed over, and is in the glove compartment.

Gerald smiles.

          GERALD
I'll let you know when I make it to my parents. I'll call again when I get my own place.

(cont'd)

(cont'd)

                    BLISS
I'll talk to you then.
Good-bye.

Gerald walks out.

                    MENARD
                (to Davis)
Now, for you.

                    DAVIS
               (to MENARD)
No, your turn.

Bliss walks away.

            MENARD AND DAVIS
                (to Bliss)
Come back here!

Bliss stops walking. She smiles.

                    BLISS
Don't ever yell at me
again.

Bliss walks away.

            MENARD AND DAVIS
                (to Bliss)
I'm sorry. I hate we
lost our baby.

Bliss stops as Menard and Davis look at each other.

Bliss turns and faces them.

(cont'd)

(cont'd)

> **BLISS**
> I apologize too. And now Menard, since you said you were going to leave too, feel free to take the sunshine BMW, and the debit card near the Beemer's keys. And just in case, Davis, if you want to leave, take the Hummer and I'll give you a debit card.

> **DAVIS**
> I'll rather drive you around while we try to make a baby that you won't lose this time because you won't be stressed out.

Menard walks out.

Bliss and Davis stare at each other.

> **BLISS**
> I'm happy.

Menard JINGLES his keys and leaves as the DOOR SLAM.

> **DAVIS**
> I told you we were meant to be together. Now, let's work on letting you rest so we can make a baby next month.

Bliss and Davis laugh and hug.

FADE OUT

Love Changes

SITCOM

MIXED: I KNEW I HAD IT

```
            #2061 HADIT
        1st. Rev. Cast and Set list
            07/20/06 MIXED
```

"I KNOW I HAD IT"

(2061)

CAST AND SET LIST

CAST:

MAE
JACKSON
WILL
SHAREE
CARLOS
PROFESSOR PAUL
VICTOR
COUSIN RUSSELL
ELEVATOR GIRL
ADMIN COCOA
EDWARD RHYMES
ASSISTANT TAMMY
SERVER
CAB DRIVER

SETS:

INTERIORS

PLEASANT-BEDROOM
KITCHEN
LIVING ROOM
ENTRY HALL
GUITERREZ & PLEASANT OUTER OFFICE HALLWAY
CARLOS'S MEETING ROOM
JACKSON'S OFFICE
CAB

EXTERIORS

PLEASANT HOUSE
RESTAURANT
RESTAURANT PATIO

Mixed: I Knew I Had It

TEASER

FADE IN:

INT. PLEASANT KITCHEN - DAY

1   It is morning and MAE, in apron, is sitting at table with SHAREE. There are oranges and apples in a bowl on the table. MAE gives an apple to SHAREE, and takes an orange for herself.

                    MAE
I know you've been sneaking junk food at school or somewhere. That's breakfast, and dinner will be special tonight.

                    SHAREE
                  (begging)
Ma, no! Please don't cook anything special.

                    MAE
I'm thinking steamed broccoli, baked and breaded asparagus, a southwestern corn medley, and grilled portobello on a nice pilaf.

JACKSON enters and stands by the door, unnoticed. He is dressed for work and carries his attache case and a manuscript. He watches silently and proudly.

                    MAE
                  (cont'd)
And you can help with the dessert substitute.

MAE gets up from the table.

                    SHAREE
Substitute? Then it won't be dessert?

SHAREE puts a scared look on her face and goes to her mom with her hands in praying posture.

                    SHAREE
                  (pleading)
I'll stop being disobedient Momma, but please don't take all the life from the last of my teenage years.
                (she giggles)

JACKSON
Good Morning ladies I love! What's the begging about?

MAE
(taking an ice cream sandwich from the freezer)
Eating the wrong sweets at the time she believes is right.

JACKSON
(tickled)
SHAREE, I know you know better.

SHAREE
Yes sir, but Momma is eating dessert for breakfast.

MAE
(rapping)
Momma is grown and SHAREE ain't on her own.

MAE begins to pop lock and robot.

JACKSON
(flat)
Time to go.

SHAREE
Be sure to grab an apple for lunch, Daddy.

JACKSON
No thanks. We have a major presentation this afternoon so we'll likely have lunch delivered to the office for everybody.

MAE rises.

MAE
You're not slick, SHAREE. Remember now, you are a child, Child.

MAE crosses to JACKSON.

                    MAE
                 (cont'd)
        It's about time for you all to get going so we
        can see what she remembers to do right today.

                    JACKSON
        She'll avoid the bad snacks alright, even if I
        have to bribe her to make sure she doesn't
        spoil my dinner again.

                    MAE
        No bribes here, Jack.

MAE walks over and kisses SHAREE on the cheek.

                    MAE
        I shouldn't have to tell you about chocolate
        again. Have a pizza face if you choose. I'll
        still love every puss- filled lump on your
        bumpy face.

                    SHAREE
        That's wrong.

                    MAE
        That's the good life. Live your life a certain
        way and resulting things are certain to come
        your way – good for good and bad for bad.

                    JACKSON
        That's for sure.

                    MAE
        Now get to school and work.

                    SHAREE
        Yes ma'am.

                    JACKSON
                 (interrupting)
                 (to MAE)
        I love you, Dear.

He kisses MAE.

SHAREE
                   (pouting)
        I was going to say that and kiss her.

SHAREE grabs her backpack and purse.

                    JACKSON
        I didn't stop you. I just moved quicker than
        you did.

                    SHAREE
                   (to MAE)
        I love you Momma. I'll do what you said about
        staying away from chocolate and other things
        that's are bad for me.

SHAREE and MAE hug. JACKSON and MAE hug and kiss. JACKSON
walks out. SHAREE follows him.

WILL and PROFESSOR PAUL are at the back door when MAE
returns to the kitchen. MAE goes to the door and opens it.

                    PROFESSOR PAUL
        So here's my artist! MAE. You've always been a
        good girl, and you're looking real good as a
        woman too.

PAUL throws his shoulders back, then offers MAE a bouquet.

                    WILL
        Hell, let us in, and take the dog on flowers
        girl.

MAE lets them inside.
                    PAUL
        Even though I'm a minister in training now, I
        still haven't lost I had . . . including my
        love for MAE Ellerby.

He holds his hand out to offer MAE the flowers.

                    PAUL
                   (cont'd)
        ... these can be for you and Mr. Pleasant.

> JACKSON
> Say they can be, huh.

> MAE
> (to JACKSON)
> I didn't hear you come in.

PAUL notices the remainder of MAE's ice cream sandwich sitting on the island. He picks it up.

> PAUL
> Lipstick says MAE likes having the good stuff early in the morning.

He takes the ice cream sandwich and eats the rest of it as JACKSON gestures with his head to MAE for her to follow him into the hallway.

INT. HALLWAY - DAY

2   As an angry JACKSON and a tentative MAE enter.

> MAE
> Sweetheart, you know she just bought him over to discuss the piece he commissioned.

> JACKSON
> Why is it whenever your so-called friend is trying to help you, I get the feeling that someone else should be around to fight when our marriage is threatened.

> MAE
> You know I keep that handled. Where is SHAREE? I thought you were taking her to school this morning.

> JACKSON
> When we walked out, Fallon was outside on the cell phone and SHAREE ran and jumped in the car with her.

> MAE
> You didn't say anything?

> JACKSON
> I said bye and do right.

                    MAE
          Sounds good to me. Now stop worrying about
          Paul. Go to work and tell me how everything
          went tonight.

                    JACKSON
          Yeah, today is going to be a good day. Now,
          where did I put the keys?

                    MAE
          Check your pockets.

He checks his pockets and then walks back into the kitchen.
He comes back out with the keys.

                    MAE
          Now go. You're already running a bit behind.

As they exit. JACKSON eagerly and MAE with fear and
trepidation.

FADE OUT:

END TEASER

ACT ONE

FADE IN:

INT. KITCHEN - TWO SHOT - WILL AND PAUL
3
                    WILL
          I should have warned you, Professor PAUL,
          JACKSON is a little insecure about being in a
          mixed marriage.

CAMERA PULLS BACK to include MAE.
                    PAUL
          Maybe that's not it. Maybe he knows she is not
          really his wife. She's really my wife. You saw
          how he reacted when he saw me. He knows.

                    MAE
          He reacted that way because I am his wife and
          you are inappropriate.

                    PAUL
          I don't want to upset you. I'm tired of hiding
          how I feel.

He starts to come towards MAE and MAE draws back her fist.

                    PAUL
                   (cont'd)
                (puts his hand up)
          Okay. I've always loved you, and you know that.

                    MAE
          I've never loved you, and you know that.
                (picks up her notebook and pen)
          Do you want me to still do the piece or not? I
          want no connection with you past this project.

PAUL goes and sits at the table, then takes an apple and
bites into it. He smiles as he chews it looking at MAE.

                    PAUL
          How much did you say it would cost now?

                    MAE
                (teeth clenched)
          A lump sum payment of $3,700 prior to
          commencement.

                    PAUL
                   (proud)
          Just double checking. I got the cashier's check
          for $5,000.

                (woefully)
          Too bad you won't see me so I can do more for
          you and your daughter.

                    MAE
          It's a fine line between a john and that Bible
          man you claim to be. How could you even think
          of a married woman the way you do and say you
          are training to lead people to God?

                    PAUL
          It's a fine line between a sinner and a saint,
          and I'm a man regardless.

                    WILL
          You sound like a reprobate-minded beggar to me.
          A confused beggar boy.

                    PAUL
          How is saying what I want equivalent to begging
          like a child?

MAE and WILL look at each other and laugh. PAUL starts to
fumble for the cashier's check. He finds it and places it
on the table.

                    PAUL
          Neither a beggar nor a boy has the money to
          make this much for a painting possible.

He exits and stumbles as he is going out the door. His coat
gets caught as the DOOR SHUTS. He opens the door and
removes his coat before he makes the DOOR SHUT again. Mae
and WILL laugh harder and MAE resumes writing.

                    MAE
          If that was all it took to get him out of here,
          you should have spoken up a long time ago. You
          could have warned me that the client was PAUL.
          Thank God his project will only require about
          five hours of work.

                    WILL
          Good. I didn't want you to turn down the work
          and I was tired of him calling me asking if I
          would get you to do a painting for his bedroom.
          Gross!

Will takes a seat at the table as MAE stops writing.

                    WILL
          Sorry about all the stuff that happened this
          morning with our arrival. You know I don't mean
          to cause trouble.

Will notices the apple PAUL bit previously.

> WILL
> (sarcastically)
> Such as catch of a man. He says and does whatever helps his pretense of holiness, tries hard to be a sugar daddy, and will not clean up after himself.

> MAE
> A funky mess. A hot blob of a whole lot of . . .

> WILL
> (Cheshire smile)
> . . . cow chips!

> MAE
> Thank you girl cause I was trying not to cuss. That's exactly it. Bull maneur.

They laugh as MAE grips her stomach and WILL wipes her eyes.

CUT TO:

INT. HALLWAY - GUITERREZ & PLEASANT'BUILDING DAY

4   This is the Same day.

ANGLE - an elevator doors as they open and JACKSON starts out.

> ELEVATOR GIRL
> Have a nice day, Mr. PLEASANT.

Suddenly JACKSON holds up his index finger and looks as though he's forgotten something. He stops and faces the elevator.

> ELEVATOR GIRL
> Yes Mr. Pleasant?

> JACKSON
> (gesturing as though he remembers)
> My apology. Have a good day Tasha.

> ELEVATOR GIRL
> You have us mixed up. I'm Tonia. Tasha is off work today. I always say the way to tell us apart is I always wear a ponytail and Tasha won't wear one for a million dollars.

JACKSON finds it funny.

> JACKSON
> Alright. What if you don't wear a ponytail, then what?

> ELEVATOR GIRL
> (a little confused)
> Not sure, but we'll figure it out when I come to work with a different hairstyle.

The elevator doors close.

INT. GUITERREZ & PLEASANT OUTER OFFICE - DAY

5   JACKSON enters. COCOA is typing at her desk which is piled high with papers.

> JACKSON
> Good morning, COCOA. How's everything this morning?

> COCOA
> Busy, Mr. PLEASANT. Mr. Guiterrez wants all these reports finished by noon.

> JACKSON
> When it rains, it hails around here doesn't it?

> COCOA
> It sure does.

> JACKSON
> When you get to a good stopping point here soon, come talk to me about what you will need from me to make sure we meet that deadline because we still have that meeting at three with another aspiring author.

> COCOA
> (looks at him with gratitude)
> Give me about 30 minutes max, 20 target and I'll be in.

> JACKSON
> Thanks. In a minute.

JACKSON walks briskly to his office.

CUT TO:

INT. RESTAURANT PATIO - DAY

6 Professor PAUL is reading from a book which is largely printed "PLEA FOR PEACE BY MYLIA JAZA". There are four other books by the Same author in view on the table.

> PAUL
> Females marching on Washington in the nude would definitely get my support for any cause just about.

> SERVER
> Are you ready to order now Professor?

> PAUL
> Well, how about ... the steak ... very well done but not burned, I just want to be sure you all kill as many parasites as possible and I don't want to see any raw meat along with my eggs sunny-side up and some of that butter rice of yours.

> SERVER
> Coming right up. I'll get you more water too.

> PAUL
> Oh, and a carafe of orange juice mixed with unsweetened tea please.

PAUL resumes reading as VICTOR walks up and takes a seat. VICTOR picks up the book that has "SEEN IN OTHER WORDS BY MYLIA JAZA" printed on it.

                    VICTOR
          Top of late morning to you Home Slice.

                    PAUL
                 (looking up)
          I would have ordered you something, but I know
          you're always late and I wanted to be sure you
          did what I needed you to do for me before I
          tried to feed you.

VICTOR shakes his head with his lips poked out and curved.

CUT TO:

INT. PLEASANT BEDROOM - DAY

7   MAE and WILL are hanging new drapery. WILL is on a ladder at the window.

8   CLOSE ANGLE ON SMILING WILL

                    MAE
          I am so happy for you and Kenny.

                    WILL
          I am happy for you and JACKSON. Hopefully my
          luck will be just as good.

                    MAE
          Luck is based on chance. Blessings based on God
          are based on guarantees.

                    WILL
          I shole know that's true. I need to be blessed
          right now to keep my balance and not fall off
          this ladder.

MAE puts her hands on the ladder to stabilize it for WILL.

CUT TO:

EXT. RESTAURANT PATIO - DAY
9
                    VICTOR
          You sent me on a heck of a morning run. Let me
          tell you how it went.

Mixed: I Knew I Had It

Suddenly a car HORN BLOWS o.s. and diverts VICTOR and PAUL.

                    VICTOR
                    (cont'd)
I just knew I had it. I was trotting along on Gigalo and a cop came along and put his siren on just as he was passing.

PAUL resumes reading "PLEA FOR PEACE".

                    VICTOR
He whipped in front of us and turned off just as the horse was throwing me off.

                    PAUL
              (shaking his head)
That's a huge foul. Glad you didn't get hurt. The papers?

Just then the SERVER walks up with PAUL's food and drink.

                    PAUL
            (hand out, looking up)
Thank you.

                    VICTOR
That looks good.

                    PAUL
I recommend you order it. My treat remember.

                    SERVER
          (putting final items down)
Another of the Same for your friend?
              (looking at VICTOR)
Same drink too – orange juice mixed with unsweetened tea?

                    VICTOR
Oh no ... just a pitcher of sweetened green tea for me.

The SERVER nods and walks away.

                    PAUL
A pitcher?

                    VICTOR
I'm thirsty! I've been working like an American
slave for you, plus was in a trotting accident.

                    PAUL
                (grinning)
Massa proud of you Jeb. Now what say you 'bout
'dem papers?

                    VICTOR
            (leaning back in seat)
I must have lost them when I fell off the
horse.

                    PAUL
                (not intimidated)
No problem. You can just go and get them after
this early brunch.

                    VICTOR
                (very firm)
Nope, I'm out of this. It's not worth the
trouble. You already know what the papers say.

                    PAUL
                (intimidated)
No, I don't.

SERVER returns with the tea for VICTOR and the check for
PAUL.

                    PAUL
                (cont'd)
                (firmly)
Thanks, that's all for now.

                    SERVER
                (walking away)
Got 'cha.

                    PAUL
The papers will show me what I need to know.
                (he twitches)

VICTOR reacts startled and reaches into his pocket and
gingerly pulls out a pocket calendar.

                              VICTOR
          Gotta note in here that today I learned you
          really are insane.

                              PAUL
                        (passes VICTOR an ink pen)
          Write what you want and think what you want. I
          believe SHAREE is the love child of JACKSON and
          MAE from way back when and they up her up for
          adoption and just got her back a few years ago
          when they got married.

                              VICTOR
                           (disgusted)
          Man, I'm losing my appetite. That child doesn't
          look a think like either one of them. Plus, MAE
          hasn't had any kids.

CUT TO:

INT JACKSON'S OFFICE - DAY

10   JACKSON is working at his desk as CARLOS enters carrying some papers.

                              CARLOS
          JACKSON, these fliers and bookmarks for
          Shakay's jazz songbook are fantastic ... thanks
          to your polish on them.
                    (he takes a seat on JACKSON'S couch)

                              JACKSON
          Hopefully they will help her avoid buying a
          bunch of books up front since money is tight
          for her right now.

                              CARLOS
          As long as there's some plan enacted to
          generate book sales, I'm perfectly content, and
          I'm sure she'll be happy too when she sees the
          extra money.

                              JACKSON
          Well, we know royalties take a moment to kick
          in, but I do plan to follow-up to see if she
          has begun taking advanced orders as scheduled.

                    CARLOS
              (smacking gum)
See what I mean ...
          (he shifts on the couch)
The greatest publishing consultant in the city is someone I know personally.

                    JACKSON
Who is that? What's the name?

                    CARLOS
         (blows and pops a tiny bubble)
JACKSON PLEASANT. The man from somewhere who stays nowhere while avoiding anywhere bad because he is going everywhere.

                    JACKSON
I can't stand him.

                    CARLOS
Sometimes I hate him too, but that's cause he works so hard he makes me tired. Your light blinds my eyes sometimes man!

                    JACKSON
You sure know how to hype a man up for the knock down Los. I know you. What's the reason for the visit?

                    CARLOS
I know we're gonna sign him either traditional or self, but I just want to be sure we get him for sure and meet the other goals for today.

                    JACKSON
Don't worry. The reports will be ready by noon at the latest, and I will go over my outline to make sure I have all the points at my fingertips for this afternoon.

                    CARLOS
              (hesitantly)
I know we're asking a lot from you and COCOA this morning. I just want to be sure everything will be okay.

JACKSON
I'm fine. COCOA's fine. We're okay.

CARLOS
I just want to be sure.

JACKSON
(realizing, eyes narrowed)
We're doing great.
(trying to laugh it off)
We'll have it done and we'll land a new author today.

CARLOS
I hope he has what it takes because not everybody who writes something is cut out to be an author – let alone one willing to generate sales on their own.

CARLOS hands him a piece of paper.

CARLOS (cont'd)
This is what EDWARD RHYMES sent to my assistant in a card with a miniature thinking-of-you cake.

JACKSON
(reading the note aloud)
I now you is always rembering pains, but I can kept you from every having harm again.

CARLOS
See what I mean . . . a damn shame coming from a grown man who brags about being a writer.

JACKSON
His work will require advanced editing and an additional proffer added to the team for now. For the long-haul, he definitely needs to take spelling and grammar classes or at least get a private tutor or study on his own.

CARLOS
Plus instruction on remembering basic business etiquette and avoiding sexual harassment.

JACKSON grabs his pen and jots a note on his presentation outline.

JACKSON
I'll be sure to mention these things tactfully today.

CARLOS
If you can, add two more slides to the presentation.

JACKSON
Will do. I'll also print the presentation hand-outs for the meeting too.

CARLOS
Is there anything you need me to do? I actually have the next couple of hours free?

JACKSON
Yes as a matter of fact. You can go through a copy of the presentation for me to let me know if anything should be changed or if anything else should be added. If no changes, you can have the presentation loaded on the projector for the meeting and I'll print the hand-outs at 1:30.

CARLOS
Perfecto Chico!

JACKSON gives CARLOS the CD with the presentation on it. CARLOS walks out the door. JACKSON walks back to his desk and sits in his chair, immediately commencing work.

FLIP TO:

INT. PLEASANT ENTRANCE HALL - DAY

11   COUSIN RUSSELL bursts in and slams door behind him.

RUSSELL
MAE!!

MAE is in living room, dusting.

                              MAE
                             (o.s.)
                In the living room! What's the matter?

INT. PLEASANT LIVING ROOM - DAY

                            RUSSELL
                          (walking in)
                The matter is fact woman, the matter is fact!

                              MAE
                Okay . . . what are you talking about?

                            RUSSELL
                The fact that I know where my money is hidden.
                I know what niche I can have on the market!

He digs into his back pocket.

                              MAE
                Now what skill or talent do you want to turn
                into a business this month?

                            RUSSELL
                     (digging in his front pockets)
                You're poking fun now, but when it kicks off
                don't still be among the disbelievers now.

                              MAE
                           (laughing)
                Alright Russ. The floor is yours.

MAE stops dusting and stands smiling attentively at
RUSSELL.

                            RUSSELL
                       (slowly and excited)
                Okay, I knew I had it on me, but I must have
                lost it. Anyway . . . paper footballs.

                              MAE
                           (confused)
                Paper footballs?

RUSSELL
Ahh! You like that too, huh? That's nostalgia baby! That's where I hook 'em on the business end!

MAE
So, you want to fold paper into triangles all day and get people to pay you for them?

RUSSELL
And pay me so they can come by and be in a paper football game or just watch one. I can see this going international!

MAE
(trying not to laugh)
Russ, people can have their kids make them paper footballs or they can make their own and thump them all day for free. Realistically, how can this become an idea that can make you money? Think.

RUSSELL props his elbow on his arm and puts his finger to his temple.

RUSSELL
Hmm. That's a good question. How can my balls be unlike anybody else's?

MAE
(joking)
Piercing or tattooing are already pretty common for genitalia. I guess you can always try to shrink one and say it's a disappearing ball.

RUSSELL laughs and lays on the couch. MAE sits in one of the recliners.

RUSSELL
I know your brain is at work over there. I'm open to ideas for doing the paper football for real.

                    MAE
          Okay . . . how about making real footballs that
          are smaller and lighter than the standard
          football, but yours are made out of recycled
          paper and are meant for indoor play without the
          threat of breaking anything.

                    RUSSELL
          See! That is straight atomic! I love it!

MAE looks up and to the left as though thinking.

                    MAE
          You can solicit individual businesses to pay
          you to collect their paper for shredding and
          recycling. Then, you can use their shredded,
          recycled paper to make your footballs and their
          money to pay for the other supplies and fund
          promotions, advertising and marketing so you
          can ultimately sell the footballs for use in
          competitive and fundraising games.

                    WILL
          Now that's what I'm talking about. I just need
          to remember that.

RUSSELL stands to his feet.

                    RUSSELL
          I can always count on you to tell me the good
          that's God, the bad that's Satan, and the ugly
          that's Medusa.

                    MAE
          Can I count on you to pick SHAREE up from
          school at 3:30 today?

                    RUSSELL
          I have one stop to make and I'll be there early
          to get her.

MAE rises and puts her hands on her hips.

                    MAE
          I don't want no mess from you Russ. I need to
          be sure you are already there when she walks
          out of the school.

                    RUSSELL
          I'm there! Early.

                    MAE
          Thank you.

                    RUSSELL
               (walking toward the door)
          You already know me and SHAREE are grabbing
          grub and won't be coming straight here, right?

MAE smiles and shakes her head.

                    MAE
          Don't spoil her too much, Russ. And remember
          she's allergic to chocolate so no chocolate,
          fudge, none of that.

RUSSELL nods his head and walks out the door.

EXT. PLEASANT HOUSE - DAY

12   RUSSELL walks to his car, opens the door, and gets in.

                    RUSSELL
          No chocolate, no fudge, no fun! Hey, she didn't
          say no ice cream or no seafood, so the show
          ain't stopped yet podna! I'll go ahead and
          shoot to be at the school at three.

FADE OUT:

END ACT ONE

ACT TWO

FADE IN:

INT. PLEASANT LIVING ROOM - DAY

13   It is a few hours later and MAE is putting some papers in her attache case as WILL enters carrying a photo album.

                        WILL
      Here's a rabbit in the hat for ya! I bet you
      forgot about this.

WILL waves the photo album.

                        MAE
               (grabbing album)
      You wish! I just quit asking about it that's
      all, because I know that sat some point you had
      lost it.

                        MAE
      It was in the safe.

They sit and begin flipping through the photos.

EXT. PLEASANT HOUSE - DAY

14   WILL and MAE are seen through the window sitting and pointing at pictures.

INT. GUITERREZ & PLEASANT - DAY

15   COCOA is sitting at her desk smiling as she hands JACKSON the comb-bound presentation hand-outs.

                      JACKSON
             (nodding his head)
    You're a gem, COCOA.

16   ANGLE - JACKSON

He FREEZES.

17   ANGLE ON COCOA

> COCOA
> (blushing)
> Hey, I'm here to make your job easier. Plus, you're the only boss I've had who works harder than I do, and I enjoy working with you.

She smiles and laughs silently.

18   ANGLE ON JACKSON

JACKSON reacts slightly and extends his hand.

19   ANGLE ON JACKSON shaking COCOA's hand.

> JACKSON
> I know I couldn't have gotten CARLOS that report on time without you. Thank you for freeing me to go over my notes. Wish me luck on this presentation.

DISSOLVE TO:

EXT. RESTAURANT - DAY

20   Its lush appearance, despite tables and chairs as far as the eyes can see, is welcoming. VICTOR and PAUL stand outside the patio gates and VICTOR gives PAUL some papers.

> VICTOR
> I don't get it.

> PAUL
> Why not? What's so hard to understand about it? It's always been this way for me.

> VICTOR
> (looking around)
> But not like this, at this type of point.

VICTOR leans in and continues to look around as though he wants to be sure no one can hear him.

> PAUL
> What's wrong with you man?

Mixed: I Knew I Had It

> **VICTOR**
> Nothing. I just wanted to be discreet when I say what I have to say.

VICTOR sits upright.

> **VICTOR**
> I think you need a professional real quick.

PAUL looks confused.

> **VICTOR** (cont'd)
> A shrink for your mind. You need to go lay on somebody's couch in a hurry.

PAUL shakes his head and laughs.

CUT TO:

21   ANGLE - CARLOS'S OFFICE

CARLOS and JACKSON walk to the table. EDWARD RHYMES, a middle-aged businessman and his assistant TAMMY, an older woman, rise as they arrive.

> **CARLOS**
> EDWARD RHYMES, meet JACKSON PLEASANT, better known
> as "The Concept Kick-Off King".

> **EDWARD**
> (shaking JACKSON's hand)
> My pleasure. I'm a big fan of yours.

> **JACKSON**
> Thank you, Mr. Rhymes.

> **EDWARD**
> Ed to my friends. This is TAMMY, my assistant. We hear your campaigns are thorough. Authors say you tell them just what to do to get anything they come up with done.

> **CARLOS**
> Right, JACKSON has the genius and will to work to get anything accomplished. Have a sit down.

EDWARD and TAMMY sit.

                    EDWARD
          Now, Carlos was telling me about your changes
          to the author requirements. He said you'd fill
          me in on 'em.

                    CARLOS
          Well, let's get the presentation going first,
          then get to that at the end.

                    JACKSON
          Either way is fine. Projector time.

                    CARLOS
          Oh!

JACKSON's eye brows raise. CARLOS reacts as EDWARD shifts
in his seat and leans to TAMMY whispering.

                    CARLOS
                    (cont'd)
          I left the presentation on my desk.

JACKSON looks as though he's not surprised or worried.

                    JACKSON
              (pulling out and issuing bound hand-outs)
          No problem. We have hand-outs prepared. Getting
          started. This is yours, TAMMY. Here you are Ed.
          And this one's for you CARLOS.

                    EDWARD
                    (interrupting)
          Prepared for whatever I see. Plan A means an
          automatic Plan B and possibly Plan C.

                    CARLOS
          The exact kind of guy you want to have on your
          team.
                    (feins punch)
          ...knocking out all complications!

JACKSON
Thanks. Now, since this will be a little less formal, let's go ahead and start with the new author requirements, then we'll go into the presentation itself.

EDWARD taps TAMMY's hand and smiles.

EDWARD
You already know curiosity had me a bit anxious for a minute there.

JACKSON
Yeah. In summary, we're requiring all authors to agree to refrain from actions that my be construed as unwanted sexual advanced or any other violation by colleagues of yours and ours. Be a professional. Date elsewhere.

CARLOS
Not you as in you specifically, but people in general.

JACKSON
And you specifically too, Ed. Another requirement is the mandatory self-education workshops to improve your spelling and general writing skills.

EDWARD
I'm a damn good writer. I don't need that!

JACKSON
(laughing nervously)
You are a visionary and you can communicate your thoughts, however, you do not write – as in spelling, structuring, punctuation and grammar – as well as one would expect after reading heavily-edited versions of your work.

CARLOS
It's all to help the author be his or her best.

EDWARD
How will requiring me to pretty much do homework helping me do more than lose time?

JACKSON
One way is when you decide to handwrite a
message, people won't think you dropped out of
fourth grade.

EDWARD giggles.

FLIP TO:

INT.   PLEASANT LIVING ROOM - DAY

22   MAE at phone.   28

MAE
I warned you...I will rip that check to shreds
if you keep on calling here and going there.

INT.   RESTAURANT - DAY

23   PAUL in phone booth.

PAUL
MAE, I'm not trying to make you mad. I want to
make you mine.

INT. PLEASANT LIVING ROOM - DAY
24
MAE
Why? Cause I'm married now! I didn't want you
when I was single! What are you holding on to?
Let it go.

MAE listens as we hear:

PAUL
(o.s.)
(filtered)
You don't remember that one summer when we were
12 and 13, our cousins kissing up front in the
car outside your aunt's house, and we kissed on
the back seat?

MAE
I remember that one smooch that lasted half a
second and I've regretted since then.

Mixed: I Knew I Had It

CUT TO:

INT. PAY PHONE - DAY

25   CLOSE SHOT - of receiver dangling as we hear:

                  MAE
                  (o.s.)
               (filtered)
       So why does that apply today?

We WIDEN SHOT and PAN UP to see PAUL rocking and struggling with the grip he has on himself. His hands are clutching his upper arms in the hug before he quickly frees himself and picks up the receiver.

                  PAUL
       I knew then I wanted to marry you. I love you.

                  MAE
                  (o.s.)
               (filtered)
       I do not love or desire you. Never have and never will.

                  PAUL
       Don't fight the feeling, MAE.

                  MAE
                  (o.s.)
               (filtered)
       PAUL, the only feeling I'm fighting is homicide.

VICTOR arrives on scene.

                  PAUL
             (seeing VICTOR)
       'Bye, MAE. I'll call you in a day or two to check on the painting. I love you.
             (hangs up phone)

PAUL steps out of the booth.

                  VICTOR
       If I wouldn't have happened to look over here, I would have left already.

                    PAUL
              (glancing at his watch)
          I'm only ten minutes late.

                    VICTOR
          But every minute of extended time counts.

                    PAUL
                    (whining)
          But every minute of extended time counts.

INT. CARLOS'S OFFICE - DAY

26   CARLOS, EDWARD and TAMMY sit as JACKSON is standing and using hand gestures.

                    EDWARD
          Sorry for the interruption, but backing up a
          little. You said I can decide whether I want
          20% royalties or 7% royalties based on
          publishing route?

At this point, a vehicle driving by is bumping bass loudly and everyone in the room bobs to the beat.

                    JACKSON
              (attempting to talk over the music)
          If I could rap, I'd say my next couple of lines
          to this beat right here.

                    EDWARD
                (bobbing his head hard)
          Maybe we can hang out one weekend and I can
          teach you a little something.

CARLOS begins to beat box the beat and tap the table.

                    EDWARD
          I can teach you that too. You got good rhythm,
          CARLOS.

                    CARLOS
          You know Mexicans got rhythm! Don't act loco,
          Chico.

They all laugh.

                    JACKSON
          But yes, Ed. You're right about what I said
          about publishing and promotion options and how
          they affect the royalties you receive.

JACKSON takes a seat.

                    ED
          So, if you all do the publishing and
          distribution and promote it, I get 7%. If you
          all distribute it and help me publish and
          promote it, I get 20%.

                    CARLOS
          And you keep all the rights when we help you
          self-publish.

                    JACKSON
          Despite the higher royalties, self-publishing
          isn't really for everybody, just like big
          publishing contracts aren't for everybody. You
          just have to decide what you are willing to do
          to generate sales after your book is published,
          and if you want to sell a million books, be
          willing to pay tens of thousands for
          advertising alone.

                    EDWARD
          I don't have to sell a million copies and I
          don't have the extra cash to buy thousands of
          books up front. I just want my book out and
          have it distributed so people can order it from
          just about anywhere. Self-publishing will be
          better for me.

FLIP TO:

INT PLEASANT ENTRY HALL - DAY

27   SHAREE bursts into the door.

                    SHAREE
                 (yelling)
          Ma... Momma, where are you?

                    MAE
                   (o.s)
                 (yelling)
        In the studio. I'll be right down.

                    SHAREE
                 (yelling)
        Did you sign that consent form for the class
        trip? Today was the last day to turn it in and
        I totally forgot.

At this, SHAREE walks forward a few steps and puts down her
backpack and purse, then walks into the kitchen. MAE begins
descending the stairs wiping her hands on a paint-stained
towel.

                    MAE
        SHAREE?

SHAREE enters through door again.

                    MAE
                 (contd)
        Hey baby. I didn't catch the last thing you
        said fully. What was it now?

                    SHAREE
                 (chewing and swallowing)
        Hi, Ma. I asked about the form for the class
        trip. It was due today.

We hear a car HORN BLOW and MAE looks curious.

                    SHAREE
        That's COUSIN RUSSELL. We're going to drop back
        by the school with the form since Teach will be
        there for a while waiting, and then we'll stop
        for ice cream and be right back here.

MAE indicates she doesn't believe SHAREE and she walks to
the window and peeks out of it.

> MAE
> (walking toward and past SHAREE)
> Okay, let me go get it for you. Don't forget your purse when you leave. And no chocolate, no fudge, home by six.

SHAREE groans.

EXT. PLEASANT HOUSE - DAY

28   RUSSELL is primping in the rearview mirror and talking to himself.

> RUSSELL
> Ladies, if there's to be an if factor, let me be the benefactor if your answer is yes.

He adjusts the volume higher on his radio.

> RUSSELL
> Will the women be ready to tussle with all the man that's RUSSELL?!!

He turns and sees SHAREE walking with a piece of paper and her purse in hand.

> RUSSELL
> Cassanova into effect beginning with her tender young teacher.

> SHAREE
> (getting in the car and shutting the door)
> Nope to whatever you're thinking. I heard you say tender young teacher. You're staying tin the car and I'll be in and out of the school before you even get your Carmex on your lips.

They laugh as RUSSELL drives away and makes his car HORN TOOT twice.

INT. PLEASANT LIVING ROOM - DAY

29   MAE stumbles going up the stairs.

                    MAE
          Okay, can you walk well enough and not break
          your neck trying to get PAUL's painting out of
          the way.

A disgusted MAE resumes her climb of the stairs, holding
onto the rail.

                    MAE
          God, make this man leave me alone, in Jesus'
          name I pray a million times.

She hears the front door shut.

                    RUSSELL
                (breathing hard)
          Quick questions and we're out of here for real
          this time.

                    MAE
                (puzzled)
          Shoot the questions. No chocolate, home by six,
          paper footballs possible.

                    RUSSELL
          Got that. Any more of your special tea, and
          what man are you trying to pray out of your
          life? I can hurt him if you need me to.

                    MAE
                (descending stairs)
          There should be one more to-go bottle stashed
          in the fridge. The nutt is PAUL, the professor
          you met not too long ago. No need to hurt him.
          God's wind will wake him up.

They walk into the kitchen. The car HORN BLOWS. MAE walks
to the refrigerator.

                    MAE
                (opening fridge and grabbing tea)
          For some reason he has taken our association
          for something far more, and it's not going to
          cause my marriage any more problems.

MAE and RUSSELL high five and walk toward the front door as RUSSELL drinks tea. He opens the door and leaves. MAE shuts the door and locks it, then pretends to be a track star as she takes off toward the stairs.

FADE OUT:

END ACT TWO

ACT THREE

FADE IN:

INT. PLEASANT LIVING ROOM - DAY

30   It is a few hours later. MAE stands wiping her hands on her paint rag. She gently picks up a large abstract painting and holds it up for evaluation.

                      MAE
Umph. I don't feel a thing, no energy, nothing from it. Perfect, for Paul.

As she lays the piece down, the DOORBELL CHIMES. MAE walks to the intercom by the fireplace, presses the button, and goes:

                      MAE
Good afternoon. May I help you?

                      SHAREE
It's me Momma. My hands are full. Cuz took me shopping.

                      MAE
               (walking toward the door)
Why did he go and do that? She's spoiled enough already.

MAE unlocks the door and opens it. RUSSELL pulls off and his HORN BLOWS twice.

                      SHAREE
           (stepping in, hitting MAE with bags)
I have stuff for you, stuff for me, stuff for Daddy, and stuff for school!

                        MAE
            You with stuff for school?

SHAREE begins putting her bags on the love seat as MAE
steps outside and looks upward. MAE then looks around and
walks back inside, shutting the door behind her.

                        MAE
            Was that really Russ or did a spaceship drop
            you off? Are you the SHAREE known as my
            daughter? Stuff for school was selected during
            a shopping spree?

                        SHAREE
            Yes ma'am, and I got three things for school!

                        MAE
                    (staggering)
            Whoa! I was amazed at the thought of just one!

SHAREE laughs as she starts going through the bags. She
pulls out a single pair of denim jeans and a matching skirt
and jacket.

                        MAE
            Good choice of coordinates. That's what you
            picked out for yourself?

                        SHAREE
            This is what I got for school. I got myself
            stuff for other places.

                        MAE
                    (laughing and picking up her painting)
            Now that's my daughter. I was worried for a
            second there.

                        SHAREE
                    (digging in bags)
            You're so funny. This is what I got for Daddy.

SHAREE hands MAE a wrapped gift.

                        SHAREE
            This one is yours.

SHAREE hands MAE a bag.

                    MAE
          We've got a lot to do, I'll tell you as we go.

MAE holds the bag open and stays focused on SHAREE awaiting direction.

                    SHAREE
          Ma, the bag, all the stuff in it, is for you.

                    MAE
                 (touched)
          This is the sweetest thing. You are so
          precious. Thank you baby.

                    SHAREE
                 (hugging MAE)
          I love you because you love me like I was your
          own. When I met my birth parents, they were
          nothing like you two.

                    MAE
                 (putting bag down)
          You've really grown a lot. I thank God for
          keeping your spirit resilient.

WILL bursts in with flowers, a stuffed animal, and a mean look. SHAREE and MAE are startled.

                    MAE
          And I pray God will put me into the habit of
          locking the door all the time.

She turns to WILL.

                    MAE
                 (cont'd)
          No offense meant, just facts wrapping up a
          previous conversation.

                    WILL
          Girl, you know I don't pay yo but no attention.

                    SHAREE
          I know somebody who got some love gifts from
          her man today.

                    WILL
                (with an attitude)
            This ain't from my man. This is from a
            psychopath.

SHAREE bucks her eyes and gathers her items as WILL starts
sitting down the gifts. She notices that SHAREE leaves the
room as will notices the painting.

                    WILL
            I like this. Is this something you're still
            working or is this drying to hang or sell?

                    MAE
            That's to get rid of the nutt job harassing me.
                (gestures with lapel)
            Professor Paul the Upcoming Pastor.

WILL and MAE both mimmick gestures of Paul and start
laughing.

                    WILL
            That's who sent me all this stuff.

                    MAE
            Paul? Thank God for turning his heart away from
            me. I'm glad you found love.

                    WILL
                (shocked)
            Love? Surely you are being sarcastic. You can't
            be serious.

                    MAE
            Now WILL you look young, but you know you were
            not born yesterday.

MAE chuckles.

                    WILL
            Naw girl, PAUL sent this stuff as a bribe to
            get me to talk to you today about him.

WILL takes a seat.

MAE
And tell me what about him? I don't want him despite what anyone can conjure.

WILL
And I can't think of nothing positive to say to any woman about PAUL as a candidate for love.

MAE
So I guess you've fulfilled your end of the deal. Conversation about PAUL is done. Let's eat some of those chocolates and see what all SHAREE has in this bag for me.

WILL
(opening candy)
You sure you're not talking about JACKSON?

MAE
Nope. I'm talking about SHAREE. Russ took her shopping after school today.

WILL
(eating and sharing candy)
Is this a weekly thing for him? Didn't he take her shopping last week? He got kids?

MAE
(eating chocolate)
No kids. Single. Working. But spoils SHAREE every chance he gets.

WILL
Now that's a man who can send me love gifts anytime!

MAE
(rising from her chair)
Girl, you so crazy!

WILL
Girl, I'm so real. He can put his shoes under my bed anytime honey. What's his name doesn't have to know a thing about RUSSELL.

MAE and WILL laugh and create a lot of girl chatter as they eat candy. WILL passes MAE the bag from SHAREE as she says:

                    WILL
I'm heading to the bathroom real quick, then I'm out with all the junk PAUL gave before JACKSON makes it home and I have to try to not mention this stuff again.

                    JACKSON
                    (suspicious)
I'm already home. What are you trying to avoid talking about again?

                    WILL
Not eating up all my chocolates, just sticking to having one or two pieces. Want some?

                    JACKSON
                (taking a couple of pieces)
Thanks. These from your new boyfriend? I see the flowers and stuffed animal.

                    WILL
              (topping the box of chocolates)
They're from an admirer who will forever be a secret cause I'm not buying what he's selling.

JACKSON finishes his first piece as WILL starts picking up her items. He pops in his last piece of chocolate as MAE goes:

                    MAE
If you're able tomorrow, can you come by in the morning to pick up the painting for PAUL so I won't have to be bothered with him anymore?

                    WILL
I will gladly see you in the a.m. I'm out. Goodnight, JACKSON.
                        (yelling)
Goodnight, SHAREE.

                    SHAREE
Goodnight. See you later.

MAE walks WILL to the door and locks the door behind her.

> JACKSON
> What's all this stuff?

> MAE
> (walking toward JACKSON)
> SHAREE was with RUSSELL and bought me back this back of stuff and you this wrapped gift.

JACKSON takes a seat.

> JACKSON
> I want to open mine now. It's been some kind of day.

> MAE
> Busier than ever at work?

> JACKSON
> Busiest, plus CARLOS left the presentation in his office after giving me a last minute assignment, and the client dragged the meeting out longer than usual. Arrgh!

> MAE
> (hugging JACKSON from behind)
> I'm sorry baby. I'm glad everything ultimately worked out. Now relax. Let's see what SHAREE got for us.

JACKSON begins removing the wrapping from the gift. As he opens it, MAE is pulling out items from her gab. SHAREE walks through eating a bag of cheese popcorn.

> SHAREE
> I came out right on time. I hope you two like what I chose for you.

> JACKSON
> (stands and hugs SHAREE)
> This is beyond thoughtful. Thank you. You didn't have to get this. You could have gotten yourself a lot of things instead of getting me this. I love you.

SHAREE
As much as you all do for me, I wanted to be sure to get you something. Russell chose your gift though. I was thinking about a necktie.

JACKSON
Necktie. I especially thank you.

MAE is placing her items back in the bag.

MAE
These were real sacrifices you made. Each item you got for us could have been something else for yourself, or several things for you. Keep maturing and one day you really will outgrow the need for being on punishments.

SHAREE
(laughing)
Must you parents remember everything?

They all laugh together as JACKSON places his arms around MAE and SHAREE. SHAREE pulls out a candy bar and takes a bite. JACKSON and MAE look at each other then look at SHAREE.

FADE OUT:

THE END

Mixed: I Knew I Had It

AUTHOR BIO
Mary Michelle Jefferson

The third of five children borne to Susie Williams Jefferson, Mary Jefferson is a native of Mississippi who has lived in Texas since first moving to Arlington in 1997.

A professional writer for most of her life, Mary wrote her first book (All About Cindy, which was eventually lost and never published) when she was just eight years old. Soonafter, she began charging fellow elementary school students who requested she complete songs, poems, stories, letters and written homework assignments for them. By high school graduation, she was earning money working in fast food, writing undergraduate research papers, and providing thesis assistance to graduate students.

By the close of her first year at Jackson State University, Mary had begun working in print media for as a copy editor for *The West Jackson Journal*. It was near the end of her second year that Mary began working as a news writer and obituary writer with Mississippi's largest newspaper, *The Clarion-Ledger*. She also freelanced briefly for the *Jackson Advocate*.

Mary completed undergraduate studies at JSU in 1996, receiving a Bachelor's of Science degree in Mass Communications. Enrolling as a double major but later downscaling to concentrate on Broadcast Journalism and instead minor in English, Mary graduated a few classes shy of receiving a second bachelor's degree. However, before relocating to Texas in 1997, Mary had also accumulated impressive broadcasting experience by working at the college's vintage jazz radio station (WJSU) and interning at the state's top television station (WLBT-3).

After arriving in Dallas/Fort Worth, Mary formed her own "communications firm" and was soon hired by the *Arlington Morning News/Dallas Morning News* as a staff writer, and by *The Dallas Examiner* as a managing editor.

In 1998, she moved from Arlington to Dallas after beginning a Finance & Accounting recruiting position with a staffing agency. For the company, she also produced a monthly newsletter and later recruited and staffed for its Healthcare division, as well as provided advertising design/copyrighting and events/program creation and implementation.

Post recruiting for another staffing firm specializing in Human Resources, Mary was introduced to the Architectural/Engineering/Construction field when she began extending marketing, administrative, technical writing, and presentation compilation services to A/E firms.

In May 2002, she enrolled at the University of Texas at Dallas to obtain a Master's degree. In December 2003, she was one of two students to be awarded a Master of Arts & Humanities from UTD. So doing, she possibly became the first African-American student to be awarded a "professional" MAH from the college's graduate program.

Since forming The Writers Consortium and The Sitting Room in 1997, Mary has completed a number of tasks through all eight of her companies.

With The Sitting Room, she completes tasks ranging from devising and implementing market research questionnaires and response analysis to data entry and website construction.

ARTiculation is the company through which she provides broadcasting services inclusive of writing and performing voice-overs for phone systems and web casts.

She has also established herself within the Metroplex community as a local artist by showing her abstract and still art work, and performing music and poetry, after booking shows in Dallas-area venues through her company PeopleWarmers.

Additionally, she helps others with: creative expression services via The Writers Consortium; support services such as image consulting, fashion and design, and diction coaching via Jefferson-Taylor; community outreach, mentoring, tutoring, and charitable donations via Life's Purpose Ministries; self-publishing assistance and self-promotions training via BePublished; and various business communications, human resources, accounting and marketing services via The Conglomerate.

All For Show: Television and Film Scripts

Under the pseudonym MYLIA TIYE MAL JAZA, Mary is the author of four works of non-fiction and fiction (poetry, translations, short stories, art work, and a novella). The titles of these works are: <u>Life Is Beautiful: La Vita E Bella</u>; <u>Life Is Beautiful: La Vita Es Hermosa</u>; <u>Seen In Other Words</u>; and <u>Plea For Peace</u>.

Other names by which Mary is known are: SAGE, among vocalists and music performance circles; and SUN CHILD WIND SPIRIT, by fellow Native Americans and visual art aficionados.

The first book she published under her birth name was actually a 2006 republishing of her great-great-uncle's 1937 work on Black-American social issues, <u>The Old Negro and The New Negro by T. LeRoy Jefferson, MD</u>.

<u>All For Show</u> is the inaugural, published presentation of a film script and a television sitcom script – both previously un-circulated, un-produced and ready for stage and recorded performance. This book is also the first of her own books published using her birth name instead of the pseudonym she chose.

All For Show: Television and Film Scripts

ISBN: 978-0-6151-6331-4